CLASSIFICATION SOCIETIES

CLASSIFICATION SOCIETIES

Edited by
JONATHAN LUX
Ince & Co., Solicitors

PUBLISHED IN ASSOCIATION WITH THE
INTERNATIONAL BAR ASSOCIATION

FOREWORD BY
THE LATE SIR RODERICK MACLEOD

LLP

LONDON NEW YORK HAMBURG HONG KONG
LLOYD'S OF LONDON PRESS LTD.
1993

Lloyd's of London Press Ltd.
Legal Publishing Division
27 Swinton Street
London WC1X 9NW

USA AND CANADA
Lloyd's of London Press Inc.
Suite 308, 611 Broadway
New York, NY 10012 USA

GERMANY
Lloyd's of London Press GmbH
59 Ehrenbergstrasse
2000 Hamburg 50, Germany

SOUTH EAST ASIA
Lloyd's of London Press (Far East) Ltd.
Room 1101, Hollywood Centre
233 Hollywood Road
Hong Kong

First published in Great Britain, 1993

British Library Cataloguing in Publication Data
A catalogue record for this book
is available from the British Library

ISBN 1-85044-491-9

Text set in 10 on 12pt Times by
Cotswold Typesetting Ltd., Gloucester
Printed in Great Britain by
WBC Print Ltd
Bridgend, Mid Glamorgan

FOREWORD

Public and political interest in the safety of ships and the protection of the environment increases continually and I believe it is both necessary and constructive to publish and exchange views on all aspects of marine safety.

The system of classification has evolved over a long period of time to set standards of strength and safety for a ship's structure and its engines (to the extent that defective engines could endanger the safety of the vessel) and to apply these standards on a consistent basis throughout the world. International classification is an essential part of the system for maintaining marine safety worldwide.

The International Classification Societies need, first, a very strong technical base, committed to developing and applying technical knowledge about structures and materials; secondly, constant feedback from inspections of ships in service; thirdly, the ability to balance the technical, commercial and political factors which are the main constituents of the safety judgment; and finally, the means and determination to apply this judgment consistently anywhere in the world, irrespective of commercial, political, technical, legal or personal pressures.

These requirements, particularly the last one, are not easy to meet. I believe that, by and large, the International Societies perform this difficult task well. As the world maritime industry is now structured, I believe that only the International Classification Societies can meet all these requirements, which are closely interconnected.

In addition to classification work, the essential work done by the International Societies on behalf of flag states merits study in its own right, although it is worth observing in passing that only the International Societies have the coverage and technical back-up to carry out this work worldwide. There are also many developing services within the boundaries of safety and quality that International Societies supply for those who want them.

World shipping is very largely a free market. The more free the market, the more difficult it is to enforce standards which to a considerable extent requires compelling people to do what they don't want to do. In the absence of effective political, legal or financial sanctions applying throughout the whole maritime industry the maintenance of acceptable standards of safety depends on the effective co-operation of a number of groups, of which the International Classification Societies are one.

The papers delivered at the International Bar Association Section on Business Law's conference in Hong Kong in 1991 show classification and the International Societies from a number of different perspectives. Taken together, I believe they make a valuable contribution to general understanding of the challenges that face the International Societies, with particular reference to the ever increasing threat of legal liability. The papers also demonstrate the need for all those who share responsibility for marine safety to work much more closely together.

3 December 1992

SIR RODERICK MACLEOD
Chairman, Lloyd's Register

PREFACE

The classification societies take centre stage when it comes to monitoring the fitness and safety of the vessels which ply the world's oceans. Their certificates are relied on by governments, underwriters, charterers, purchasers and others as evidence that the vessels are fit and, by and large, the classification societies have a commendable record.

However, classification societies are not immune from mistakes and there is increasing concern that, with growing competition between the classification societies, standards, at least in some of the lesser-known societies, are dropping. Highlighting this concern, a recent article commented:

> One of the most important topics which has occupied the minds of London underwriters over the past year has been their attempt to impose pressure on classification societies to remove sub-standard ships from their registers. There has been a concerted effort by insurers to improve vessels' standards which have shown a marked decline in recent years. The reason for the increasing numbers of sub-standard vessels is not difficult to find. The world fleet is in need of some urgent replacement of tonnage as the average age of vessels advances. The principal reason for this is, as a result of the increase in world trade, shipping activity is showing a marked upturn and many older vessels are being utilised and released from lay-up berths.

The contributions to the present text were initially prepared as papers which were presented at a meeting of the Section on Business Law's Maritime and Transport Law Committee (Committee A) of the International Bar Association (IBA) in Hong Kong in late 1991. In order of appearance in the present text we have (i) Mr Boisson, legal advisor to Bureau Veritas, who examines the legal position of classification societies in American, English and French law; (ii) Mr Hutchison, the former Deputy Chairman of Lloyd's Register, the oldest and largest classification society, gives an interesting account of the practical and political considerations; (iii) Mr Ulrik of the Danish Shipowners' Defence Association pulls no punches when it comes to setting out the underwriters' perspective; (iv) my then Hong Kong resident partner, Mr Moore, sets out the English and Far East perspective which, at the time the paper was prepared, rested with the *Morning Watch* decision exonerating the classification society from responsibility; (v) Mr Starer, a partner in the New York law firm Haight Gardner Poor and Havens, argues cogently that classification societies should no longer be permitted to shield themselves from liability for negligence in the rendering of their services; and (vi) two German lawyers, Dr Breitzke of the Hamburg law firm Lebuhn and Puchta and Dr Brandi of the Hamburg law firm Weiss and Hasche set out the rival arguments for and against liability of classification societies.

Whilst different views are put forward on the issues of role and responsibility, one point is quite clear—namely, that the growing concerns felt by the world's shipping community will have to be addressed. One possibility appears to be compulsory membership of the International Association of Classification Societies (IACS) and the 'policing' of quality control by IACS and the power to impose sanctions where standards are not met. If self-policing fails then there will be growing pressure for redress from the civil courts and, in this regard, there is an interesting development in the form of the very recent English High Court decision in *The "Nicholas H"* (see Case Digest in Appendix 1). In brief, on the trial of a preliminary issue, the court held the defendant classification society could be liable to the plaintiff cargo owners in circumstances where the vessel had sunk a matter of days after leaving the load port, having been certified as fit for the voyage by the attending classification society surveyor.

This appears to be the first English case in which a classification society has been held to owe a duty of care capable of giving rise to a liability in damages. The facts of this case were of course somewhat extreme but now that the door to civil liability is ajar, others can be expected to push.

Ince & Co.

JONATHAN LUX
Committee A Vice-Chairman

CONTENTS

ABOUT THE IBA, THE SECTION ON BUSINESS LAW, AND ITS MARITIME AND TRANSPORT LAW COMMITTEE

The International Bar Association (IBA) is the world's foremost international association of lawyers, with a membership of over 15,000 individual lawyers in 163 countries as well as 142 Bar Associations and Law Societies. Its principal aims and objectives are:

- — to encourage the discussion of problems relating to professional organisation and status;
- — to promote an exchange of information between legal associations worldwide;
- — to support the independence of the judiciary and the right of lawyers to practise their profession without interference;
- — to keep abreast of developments in the law, and to help in improving and making new laws.

Above all, it provides a forum for the dissemination of specialist knowledge on all areas of law as well as promoting contact and interchange between lawyers throughout the world.

SECTIONS AND COMMITTEES

The IBA has three Sections: the Section on Business Law, the Section on General Practice, and the Section on Energy and Natural Resources Law.

The Section on Business Law is the largest Section, with over 11,500 members. It aims to promote exchange of information and views amongst members as to laws, practices, and procedures affecting business, financial, and commercial activities throughout the world.

The Section operates through 28 specialist Committees, of which Committee A (Maritime and Transport Law), is one of the larger with 1,000 members.

Further details of the IBA are available from: 2 Harewood Place, Hanover Square, London W1R 9HB. Telephone: +44 (0)71 629 1206. Fax: +44 (0)71 409 0456.

INTRODUCTION TO COMMITTEE A

The Committee on Maritime and Transport Law (Committee A) of the Section on Business Law (SBL) of the International Bar Association (IBA) consists of 1,000 maritime and land transport law specialists from over 60 countries. The Committee maintains links with leading international maritime and transport organisations, has an active publishing programme, meets annually in conjunction with the Biennial Conference of the SBL or the Biennial Conference of the full IBA and participates in the IBA's regional conferences.

At each annual conference, Committee members deal with a variety of timely topics, present reports on national and regional developments of interest to practitioners, and examine at least one major topic in depth.

We are very pleased that Lloyd's of London Press has chosen to publish the papers from Committee A's session entitled "The Role and Responsibility of Classification Societies" which was presented during the SBL's Hong Kong Conference in October 1991. We thank the contributors for their enthusiastic participation and congratulate them on the high professional standard exhibited by their papers.

New York,
August 1992

LENNARD K. RAMBUSCH
Committee A Co-Chairman

TABLE OF CASES

FRANCE

GERMANY

TUNISIA

UNITED KINGDOM

UNITED STATES

TABLE OF STATUTES

TABLE OF CONVENTIONS

CHAPTER 1

THE LIABILITY OF CLASSIFICATION SOCIETIES IN THE MARINE INDUSTRY CONTEXT

There are many reasons connected with changes in the maritime world over the last 15 years. Two factors which have altered the working environment of classification societies are:

— The economic crisis in shipping which has intensified competition among shipowners, forcing them to use older ships, and to cut operating costs to the bone. Any effects on maintenance and servicing are obviously to the detriment of safety at sea.

— A greater awareness of marine conservation issues which has arisen from a series of major ecological disasters, such as oil spills. At present, the typical reaction is to seek compensation at any cost. Plaintiffs tend to sue not the person responsible, but whoever can pay however minimal or peripheral his role in the accident. Such an attitude appears to be the result of the generalisation of insurance, which has perverted the mechanisms of the law of tort: a judge often tends to find against an insured person rather than the actual bearer of liability. The wish to ensure that victims receive compensation encourages him to try and find the money, and thus insurance, rather than the actual causal fault.

Other reasons, peculiar to classification societies, have contributed to the increase in the number of lawsuits against them.

To begin with, such bodies are clearly working under increasingly difficult conditions. The time is long gone when there were only a few large societies worldwide with international reputations which established and supervised the rules of maritime safety in the noticeable absence of state intervention. At present, there are more than 40 classification societies in the world, which are in competition with each other. This situation may to some extent have encouraged a tendency to regard the services involved in the classification of maritime vessels and equipment as commonplace. The result has been decline in the quality of service by some unscrupulous societies.[1] The phenomenon has also been accentuated by the carelessness of certain maritime insurers who do not always

1. To halt this trend, societies belonging to the International Association of Classification Societies (IACS) set up an ambitious quality assurance programme for their services in 1990.

make a proper distinction between trustworthy classification societies and organisations that may be described as societies 'of convenience'.

Over the years, classification societies have also diversified their services to keep pace with changes in the maritime world and to respond more effectively to their customers' needs. Instead of confining their work to the mere provision of information on the quality and reliability of ships, they have become promoters of international maritime technical regulations. Technical assistance and consultancy have assumed a growing importance in their services so that, whenever matters of safety are involved, they are sometimes regarded as jacks of all trades.

This confusion about their role in the maritime sector has been maintained and reinforced by their near-neurotic reluctance to communicate, which has led to misunderstandings and incomprehension, leading to disputes as to the nature and scope of their obligations and responsibilities. In certain cases, classification agencies have even been made the scapegoat for the evils and defects of the whole maritime safety system.[2]

It is not necessary to paint the picture any blacker. A classification society is not a legally irresponsible entity: like any professional purveyor of goods or services it is committed to certain obligations and may meet claims of liability if it fails to comply with them. Such liability, however, raises three kinds of questions:

- How do the courts see the role and obligations of classification societies, and their consequent liabilities? Are there similarities or divergencies among the national legal systems of the UK, France and the USA in the exact assessment of their functions?
- How do judges see classification society activities? Are they mere purveyors of services like anyone else, no more than information agencies, or can they claim a special usefulness, a particular justification, a specific professional role, and consequently enjoy favoured treatment compared with common law requirements?
- Ultimately, what is the outlook for such institutions? Sooner or later, will they disappear under pressure of the growing burden of responsibility on their surveyors. Or, given the contribution they can make to safety of life at sea and conservation, can national judicial authorities grant them some degree of special status, or at any rate a benevolent attitude, to ensure greater effectiveness?

This matter of classification society liability will be examined from the dual viewpoint of their responsibility towards their customers, and towards third parties.

2. E. Langavant and P. Boisson: 'L'affaire du naufrage de la drague Cap de la Hague et le problème de la responsabilité des sociétés de classification', DMF 1981, pp. 131–45.

CLASSIFICATION SOCIETY OBLIGATIONS TO CLIENTS

Before considering the details of the contractual liability of classification societies, and the means of curtailing its effects by the use of limitation clauses, two preliminary questions arise: who calls upon their services, and in which form are contractual commitments entered into?

Originally, classification was carried out for the sole use of insurers and marine charterers. They were notified of the class on a confidential and personal basis on payment of an annual subscription to the Register. When the concept of duration of class was introduced, shipowners wishing to keep an eye on the construction of their vessels, and subsequently to survey them, became the main clients of classification societies. They were followed by shipyards, vitally interested in the technical rules and recommendations drawn up by classification societies from the middle of the nineteenth century.[3]

Nowadays, it is not always easy to define the exact scope of contractual commitments because classification society clients change during the life of the vessel. This process starts on delivery which in most cases involves transfer of ownership. The question is whether the society, whose contract up to that point has been solely with the shipyard, can impose the same contractual stipulations on the shipowners when they take possession of his ship. This is indeed the case if there is a tripartite contract among the interested parties, or if the society has taken care to sign another classification contract with the shipowner, who becomes a new client.

Similarly, the purchaser of a ship cannot claim *per se* any contractual bond with the classification society prior to delivery. In the absence of any particular agreement among the parties, the classification society's client at the time of sale remains the vendor, under the terms of the existing contract.[4]

What form do contractual obligations take? A recent survey among members of the International Association of Classification Societies (IACS) has revealed the use of quite a wide variety of documents: request forms accompanied by contractual clauses, standard contracts, general conditions appended to the contract or incorporated in it by reference. Whatever procedure is adopted, such documents, in order to be legally valid (in other words, to reflect the wishes of the parties) have to be accepted by the client. The client's consent may be tacit, but some classification societies ensure that it is expressed by a letter of acceptance with signatures at the bottom of a form, etc. This is not mere officiousness: as it provides a more secure legal relationship and greater contractual freedom. Above all, it helps to avoid subsequent lengthy arguments about the effects and terms of the contract.

3. *Bureau Veritas 1828/1978, 150 ans d'histoire*. Booklet published to mark the society's one hundredth and fiftieth anniversary.

4. *Case of the Bdabda ex Atho*, Paris Commercial Court, 17 May 1983 (verdict unpublished).

Content of contractual obligations

The fundamental source of the obligations of a classification society is the contract between it and the shipowner or shipbuilder. Failure to perform such obligations involves its liability. Under French law, courts apply article 1147 of the Civil Code, which renders any contracting party liable for defaults and negligence committed in the course of performance of the obligations incumbent on him. UK and US law employ the doctrine of breach of contract in awarding damages to the aggrieved party.

As mentioned above, contracts in this area may take various forms. French doctrine suggests adding classification rules, which not only provide technical recommendations on strength and safety for shipbuilding, but are often referred to in the various operations involved in assigning and maintaining ship class.

> Default exists only if the surveyor fails to comply with the rules, since rules accepted by shipowners form the law for the parties, and govern the extent of the society's obligations.[5]

Rules also comprise a number of stipulations which the client must observe with regard to the classification society. This explains why the obligations of each party need to be examined in turn.

Classification society's obligations

Such obligations are normally set out explicitly in the contract. They may also exist implicitly, for example when the law acknowledges the existence of a duty of care for certain professionals. Finally, there is the question as to whether obligations can arise outside the contract.

Explicit obligations

Everything here depends on the type of contract entered into with the client. Classification societies offer several types of services, including classification, delivery of statutory certificates, and various forms of technical assistance. There are outline or ordinary contracts for each situation and these always state the limits on services. As regards classification, for instance, services usually comprise examination and approval of drawings, inspection of materials, survey of construction in the shipyard, and attendance at ship trials. On completion of these operations the society undertakes to issue the classification certificate to publish the name of the vessel in its register, and finally to carry out periodical surveys in order to check that requirements for maintenance of class are being met.

The courts trying to determine the actual bearing of obligations examine contracts very carefully. In the case of the trawler CT2, the Appeal Court in Tunis made a clear distinction between types of certificates. It concluded that an

5. Georges Ripert: *Droit Maritime*, Tome 1, Paris 1929, p. 390.

attestation by Bureau Veritas (BV), issued after a specifically restricted survey with a view to delivery of seaworthiness certificates, could not have the same legal bearing as a comprehensive survey carried out for classification purposes.[6]

In a summary judgment handed down on 17 April 1991 by the thirty-second Judicial District Court of the State of Louisiana, the American Bureau of Shipping, the (ABS) was considered to be under no obligation to the owner of an offshore barge on which a faulty piece of equipment, a capstan, had caused serious injury to a foreman. The argument rested on the fact that the capstan is not covered by ABS classification rules:

> The capstan is not part of the vessel's propulsion equipment and is therefore classified as 'non-essential' machinery, which places the capstan outside the scope of ABS rules. Thus, ABS had no duty to review the design of the capstan nor to survey the capstan.[7]

Disputes between classification societies and their clients generally arise from misconstruing the nature of service, or a misconception of their remits. A classic example is when a shipowner believes that a simple survey statement will provide him with cover against all mistakes and poor workmanship committed by the shipyard and its subcontractors. The court exonerates the classification society on the grounds that: "the basic assignment of the society was to issue a national loadline certificate . . . and was not expected to approve drawings, nor check conformity of construction, nor attend tests."[8]

French case law has traditionally regarded classification societies as information agencies, and has laid down several hypotheses to define their services: sales contract, hiring contract, agency contract.[9] Whatever option is adopted, the nature of their obligations in French law is always the same. Since a decision of the Paris Court on 16 November 1927,[10] the obligation weighing on any information agency is an obligation of means and not of results, a general obligation to act with caution and care, not to perform a given act.[11] This choice is explained by the uncertain nature of the activity performed.

Under French and UK law, the mechanism for involvement of contractual liability is quite straightforward: the client does not need to prove default. He needs only to establish the existence of the contract, demonstrate that the classification society has failed to fulfil its commitments, and that failure to comply with such obligations has caused him injury. The society will thereupon be required to prove that it has applied all the skill and care needed for the proper

6. The CT2 case led to three judicial findings, exonerating Bureau Veritas: Tunis Civil Court, 15 June 1953; Tunis Appeal Court, 23 February 1955; Tunis Supreme Court, 10 April 1961. Only the decision of the Appeal Court has been published, in *Le Droit Maritime Français* 1956, p. 87, and Le Jurisclasseur Périodique 55, II, pp. 8809–8810.

7. 32nd Judicial District Court, State of Louisiana, *Lise Marie Neil* v. *Teledyne Movible Offshore*.

8. Saint Malo Commercial Court, 2 July 1991, Jusant case (verdict unpublished).

9. T. Gandolfpo: 'Bureau Veritas, procédures de classification et de contrôle. Aspects techniques et juridiques', *Mémoire DESS des Transports Maritimes*, Aix University, 1982, p. 70.

10. *Jurisclasseur Périodique* 1928, p. 53.

11. A. Tune: 'La distinction des obligations de résultats et des obligations de diligence', *La Semaine Juridique*, 1945, I, p. 449, nos. 2–6.

performance of its services. It can be fully exempted from such a requirement only by establishing an act of God, or the act of a stranger, or partly, if there is default by the plaintiff.

Implicit obligations

UK and US law require professionals to observe certain implicit obligations of care, allowing clients to sue them for liability and obtain compensation in cases of injury.

POSITION IN UK LAW

The position of the UK courts can be summarised by the proposition that they require professional men to possess a certain minimum degree of competence and to exercise reasonable care in the discharge of their duties.[12] In any contract with a professional man there is, generally implied by law, a term that he will exercise reasonable skill and care. In other words, he must prove this in order to discharge the implied contractual obligations.[13] The behaviour of the professional is assessed against a standard of skill and care, defined as 'that degree of skill and care which is ordinarily exercised by reasonably competent members of the profession, who have the same rank and profess the same specialisation (if any) as the defendant'.[14]

English case law comprises very few verdicts involving classification societies. The following principles have been determined regarding an onshore surveyor:[15]

- The standard required is that of the ordinary skilled man exercising the same skill as himself. He is variously described in the cases as 'reasonably skilled', 'competent', 'prudent', or 'an average surveyor'. When a limited task is required, for example a brief survey, the standard is lower. It must be determined having regard to the circumstances and knowledge current at the time when the surveyor was required to carry out his instructions. The court must be careful not to be wise after the event.
- Evidence of the standard is determined by reference to the general practice and knowledge of surveyors.
- The standard of reasonable care and skill allows for a margin of differing opinion and even a degree of error.

POSITION IN US LAW

US courts have established similar case law with regard to professionals supplying goods and services. The 'Ryan warranty' was the work of the Supreme Court in the case of *Ryan Stevedoring Co* v. *Pan Atlantic Corp*. The case involved

12. R. M. Jackson & J. L. Powell: *Professional negligence* (Sweet & Maxwell, London 1982), p. 4.
13. *Ibid*. p. 8.
14. *Ibid*. p. 12.
15. *Ibid*. p. 91–95.

a dispute between a handling agent and a shipowner who had been ordered to pay compensation for bodily injury to a docker who had been injured because of badly stowed cargo. The Supreme Court found the contractor liable under its stevedoring contract: 'It held that where a contractor undertakes to provide a service, implicit in the contract is a warranty that the service will be provided in a workmanlike manner.'[16] The Ryan doctrine has been extended within the maritime field to cover the activities of shipowners, painters, repair yards, launch operators, pilots and towing companies.

Does this precedent apply to classification societies? One argument which militates in its favour is that in general, by agreeing to survey and classify a ship a classification society contractually undertakes to provide services to a shipowner. An 'inescapable element' of this contract is the implied warranty to perform the survey in a safe and competent manner, so as not to expose the shipowner to risk of loss or liability to others.

US courts, however, adopt a different line of argument and consider that the classification society is not bound to an implied warranty of workmanlike performance towards his clients. In the Tradeways II case,[17] the Southern District Court of New York based its verdict on several factors in setting aside the Ryan doctrine:

— The burden of ensuring the seaworthiness of a vessel must ultimately rest upon the shipowner or charterer.
— A classification society rarely, if ever, would create hazards or defects by its functions and activities.
— Unlike a stevedore and other similar service contractors, a classification society is functionally incapable of repairing or rectifying defects or hazards caused by itself or others. Virtually all a society can do is observe and report to the owner, whatever its inspections reveal.

In *The Amoco Cadiz* case,[18] Judge McGarr also refused to apply the Ryan doctrine to ABS operations for the periodical survey of the steering gear, failure of which led to the disaster.

This court finds that Amoco is not entitled to indemnity under the doctrine of Ryan because:

— Amoco negligently failed to fulfil several of its duties with respect to the seaworthiness of the ship
— Amoco played a part in approving the design and the construction of the vessel
— the workmanship which caused the injuries for which Amoco had been found liable was not entrusted solely to ABS.

16. *Ryan Stevedoring Co* v. *Pan-Atlantic Corp.*, 350 US 124, 1956, AMC 9 (1956).

17. *Great American Insurance Co* v. *Bureau Veritas*, 338 F Supp. 999, 1972, AMC 1455 (SDNY), 1992 aff'd, 478 F 2d 235, 1973, AMC 1755 (2nd Cir. 1973).

18. *In Re Oil Spill by the Amoco Cadiz*, 1986, AMC 1945, 1951–54.

Concurrent liabilities

When damage results from failure to comply with a contractual obligation attributable to a classification society, can its client claim tort liability?

On this point French law is firm: the Supreme Court of Appeal clearly laid down the principle of 'non-concurrence' in that when the conditions exist that confer a contractual character on liability, the victim cannot, even when it would be in his interest, invoke the rules of tort liability.[19]

In UK law it is a common practice to plead professional negligence by a client against his surveyor, both in contract and in tort.[20] The possible differing consequences of the two bases of claim in the context of professional negligence by a classification society, however, remain to be explored.

To the extent that US law still allows for contractual and tort liability to run concurrently, it appears a suit in tort will no longer be permitted on a claim for economic loss only arising out of a commercial contract whether or not the claimant has a contract with the alleged wrongdoer. In any event it has been concluded that 'an indemnity obligation founding in tort is unlikely to be imposed on a ship classification society because, as a matter of fundamental legal principle, imposition of a duty to indemnify on the ship classification society would unacceptably relieve the owner of his non-delegable duty to maintain a seaworthy vessel.[20]

Shipowner's obligations

The classification contract is a legal instrument that generates obligations; for the society classing the vessel, and also for the shipowner requesting its services. Such obligations are provided for in the contract and by classification rules. Case law has also imposed certain duties on the clients of classification societies.

Formal obligations

As pointed out, these appear in nearly all classification society contracts, general conditions and rules. The most important ones comprise:

- to maintain the ship in the condition recorded on the occasion of the last survey and until the next one;
- to notify classification surveyors of any defect revealed during the construction of the ship, and to propose compensations, consolidations or alterations, in order to remedy them;
- to inform the society whenever the ship is in dry dock or on the slips, where the outside of the hull and associated items can be inspected;

19. Cass. Civ. 11 January 1922, Serey 1924, 1, 105 and note Demogue, *Dalloz* 1922, 1, 16. Cass. Civ., 16 November 1965, Dalloz 1966, 61.

20. *Great American Insurance Co* v. *Bureau Veritas*, 338 F Supp. 1012, 1015, 1972 AMC and 1472, 1476–77.

— in the event of the ship running aground, or other damage to the hull, main engines and auxiliaries, which affect or could affect the class, to request the society to have the ship surveyed;
— in the case of alterations or maintenance work affecting class to submit applications promptly so that the surveyor can check the scale of the work undertaken.

It was precisely for this failure to comply with the last obligation that the owner of *Compass Rose III* was found guilty by the French courts. The BV surveyor had been arraigned for granting the ship an extension of class for navigation on the high seas, whereas the original class had been confined to coasting, and this had been done without making a further survey of the ship. Neither the lower court judge nor the Court of Appeal[21] treated the surveyor's lack of curiosity as a criminal fault. However, they found the shipowner guilty of infringing the provisions on safeguarding human life at sea and of 'imprudence in accepting changes made in the *Compass Rose III* without checking the effects on safety'. The judges considered that the shipowner had concealed the alterations from the classification society, implying that there had been a simple change of equipment.[22]

Implicit obligations

For the shipowner, such obligations include keeping his vessel seaworthy. For the shipyard, they involve the builder's responsibility for latent defects predating delivery of the ship.

LATENT DEFECT GUARANTEE

In French law, a classification society cannot be held responsible for a latent defect which may have escaped its attention during construction. The shipyard remains fully responsible for its work and the law does not allow it to delegate such liability to another party. On several occasions, case law has recalled this principle to the extent that the classification society does not accept any special obligations to guarantee the seaworthiness of the ship.[23]

SEAWORTHINESS GUARANTEE

There is usually considerable confusion about the concept of 'seaworthiness'. Is a classed ship seaworthy? Does the classification certificate provide proof of the

21. *Compass Rose III Case*. Avranches Court, 12 January 1982. Caen Appeal Court, 12 January 1983 and Cour de Cassation, Criminal Court, 8 October 1985 (decisions unpublished).
22. In fact, this involved the installation of a 12 metre derrick on the ship's afterdeck.
23. Cf Brest Commercial Court, 26 December 1976, RIDM T 29, p. 746; Dunkirk Commercial Court, 14 May 1923, DMF 1923, DMF 1923, 294; Marseilles Commercial Court, 6 January 1978, DMF 1978, 510.

shipowner's care in this area? Can the owner delegate all responsibility for complying with his obligations to the classification society? The answers provided by national legal systems seem fairly convergent.

As regards classification and seaworthiness, under US law, it is quite clear that classification does not prove the seaworthiness of the vessel. *The Negus* case[24] is concise on that point:

'Classification does not make a vessel seaworthy, nor the absence of it make her unseaworthy.' Further, the term 'seaworthiness' has been so diluted in US law that it includes all sorts of items that are not within the duty of classification societies. In *The Argo Merchant* case[25] the court found the ship unseaworthy because she did not have a current pilot chart, the gyrocompass was not corrected and the RDF had failed because water had corroded connections in the junction box. Due to the overuse of the word 'seaworthiness' in the USA, some classification societies have dropped the term from their vocabulary.

UK case law has undergone a remarkable turnaround in this respect. For a long time it regarded certificates delivered by classification societies as authentic in establishing the shipowner's 'due diligence'. The owner could not be held 'responsible for an error committed by a classification society like Lloyd's, which occupies a public and quasi-judicial position',[26] or because requiring more than a certificate 'would involve a withdrawal beyond the diligence to be expected from a traditional employer'.[27] Courts have now completely changed their attitude: on 13 December 1961, the House of Lords, in *The Muncaster Castle* case,[28] considered that the surveyor's negligence could in no way relieve the owner of his responsibilities. On 4 June 1962, the High Court decided that the certificate was no more than a presumption of due diligence, which can be overturned by proof of negligence by the classification society.[29]

In France, case law adopts similar solutions regarding unseaworthiness and latent defects:

— As regards seaworthiness, the courts consider that certificates issued by a classification society have no absolute value and constitute a simple presumption.[30] A decision of the Appeal Court in Rouen,[31] however, admitted the good state of seaworthiness of a ship built in a reputable shipyard, which had suffered no serious damage since commissioning, and which had been accepted without reservations by competent classification bodies.

24. *The Negus Mowinckel* v. *New York Bermudez Co*, 2 May 1923, District Court, S.D. New York.

25. *In the matter of the complaint of Thebes Shipping Inc as owner of the ST Argo Merchant*. District Court, S.D. New York, 7 Feb. 1980.

26. 456 [1927] 2 KB 462.

27. [1952] 2 Lloyd's Rep. 105, 130.

28. [1961] 1 Lloyd's Rep. 57, DMF 1963, p. 246.

29. [1962] 1 Lloyd's Rep., p. 538 confirmed by House of Lords, 15 September 1963.

30. Paris, 12 December 1972, BT 1973, p. 72. In contrast, cf Paris Commercial Court, 9 May 1972, DMF 1972, p. 559.

31. *Gazette du Palais 26*, 26 November 1972, p. 7.

— Numerous legal decisions on latent defects acknowledge that surveyors' certificates delivered to shipowners prior to departure noting the good condition of the ship, in a sense constitute mere presumption which can be overturned by proof to the contrary.[32] For example, the certificate issued by BV does not relieve the owner of the need to exercise supervision and maintain equipment subject to wear and tear.[33] Similarly, the technical survey of the ship and its various installations does not relieve the owner of the need to exercise permanent vigilance.[34] Finally, it should be noted that the absence of certificates creates a presumption of unseaworthiness which can be overruled by proof to the contrary.[35]

As regards the shipowner's fundamental obligations a brief survey of US, UK and French case law shows that a shipowner has a fundamental obligation to keep his ship seaworthy. This expression means not only that the condition of the ship must be such that it can face the risks normally foreseeable, but also that it must be in a position to ensure the transportation of cargo and passengers in complete safety.

The long-established obligation to keep a vessel seaworthy has influenced considerably judges in their assessment of the legal relations that must prevail between the owner and the classification society. *The Tradeways II* and *The Amoco Cadiz* cases illustrate this tendency. The owners and insurers of *The Tradeways II* were trying to use the presumption of unseaworthiness to prove the classification society negligent. Generally, where a vessel is lost under ordinary conditions with no other explanation, US law presumes that she was unseaworthy.

In order to bring this presumption to bear against the defendant, the plaintiff had to establish a number of difficult facts, the first of which was to show that the ship was unseaworthy when it departed Antwerp and secondly, that a classification society bears the responsibility for the seaworthy condition of a vessel that it surveys.

After noting, on examination of the reports from legal experts, that *The Tradeways II* was seaworthy, the judge declared that the presumption could be borne only against the owner, bareboat charterer and possibly the builder, but not against the classification society ' which did nothing more than to classify a ship that proves to be unseaworthy'.

Even more interesting were his remarks on the owner's obligations:

— There is 'a longstanding policy or rule that the owner of a ship has a non-delegable duty to maintain a seaworthy vessel'.
— If a contrary principle were accepted, 'this, in turn, would have the effect

32. Cour de Cassation, 23 July 1951, BT 1951, p. 640; Paris, 24 October 1955, BT 1955, p. 327; Le Havre Commercial Court, 25 August 1978, DMF 1979, p. 103.
33. Marseilles Commercial Court, 9 September 1975, Revue Scapel 1973, p. 54.
34. Aix, 15 March 1978 (unpublished).
35. Rennes, 18 February 1974, DMF 1974, p. 335.

of leaving injured seamen and shippers with no effective remedy in most cases'.

— In theory, recognition of an action against a classification society would produce several undesirable effects. One of these would be to place the ultimate responsibility for seaworthiness on an organisation which has contact with the vessel for only brief annual periods, whereas the owner, who is always 'present' in respect to his vessel, would elude liability in many cases. Second, this right of action would have the effect of making the classification society an absolute insurer of any vessel it surveys and certifies. Not only is this liability not commensurate with the amount of control that a classification society has over a vessel, it is also not in accord with the intent of the parties, the fees charged or the services performed. Further, by making classification societies the effective insurers of nearly all seagoing vessels, insurance companies might be putting themselves out of business.

Finally, the court rejected the argument that BV had failed in its duty to use due care to detect and warn of hazards since the owner had learnt, through other channels than classification, of defects in the ship but had not proceeded to correct them.

The same line of argument was adopted by Judge McGarr in *The Amoco Cadiz* case:

> With respect to the surveys by ABS, this Court notes that ABS will not be held liable for failing to disclose those defects and problems with Amoco Cadiz about which Amoco knew. With respect to those problems, it cannot be said that Amoco relied upon ABS' undertaking. Moreover, to hold ABS liable in that situation would be contrary to public policy. A shipowner who has knowledge of problems with its vessel cannot escape liability for failing to correct those problems on the basis that a classification society hired to survey the ship did not detect those defects.

From this it is possible to conclude that the contract and rules play a decisive part in defining the obligations of classification societies and their customers. It is also these documents that usually lay down restrictions as to the involvement of such societies' liabilities and the amount of compensation payable in cases of negligence. It is also important to weigh up the bearing of such provisions.

Legal validity of limitation of liability clauses

For a considerable time, nearly all classification societies have inserted limitation clauses in their contracts. What form do they take? What is their justification? These preliminary questions have to be answered before considering the attitude of the law towards them.

Examination of limitation clauses and their justification

There is no single standard limitation clause common to all classification societies. Each society, as it sees fit, uses the most suitable means of avoiding or limiting its liabilities. However, such stipulations can be divided into several categories.

Types of clause

Originally, there were non-liability and disclaimer clauses, under the terms of which classification society operations could not be the subject of legal action, or their pecuniary liability involved, whether because of the opinion expressed about ships or because of errors or omissions in their registers, or due to errors, faults or negligence by their agents.

Liability limitation clauses appeared a few years ago. Fearing a rejection in principle of non-liability clauses by the courts, some classification societies have accepted possible compensation for their errors under certain conditions, the amount of such indemnifications naturally varying from one society to another.

Another way of avoiding liability is 'hold harmless clauses', aimed at covering all actions not attributable to the society through its sole negligence. Use is also made of time-limitation clauses, which place an expiry date on legal action, and compulsory jurisdiction and arbitration clauses.

Justification for exclusion and limitation clauses

The sharpest criticism is naturally aimed at non-liability clauses. Classification societies offer professional services and in so doing must bear the consequences of their actions: they should be treated as responsible, if they fail to obey professional rules.[36]

Partisans of non-liability clauses put forward the following arguments[37]:

- Classification, which is the expression of the degree of confidence placed by the society in the ship, is a simple opinion reflecting only a strictly personal assessment, and therefore subject to discussion by interested parties.
- Human error remains possible, and there has never been any question of demanding that a technical advisor (also the role of the classification society), however highly qualified, should, on his own responsibility, guarantee the accuracy of the information he supplies and the infallibility of the opinion he expresses.
- Classification of a ship involves payment of only a modest fee. The society cannot be expected to supply, for such a low price, a completely accurate opinion on the value of the ship.

Beyond this doctrinal squabble, what is the attitude of the courts?

36. Bonecasse: *Traité de droit commercial maritime*, Paris, Sirey 1912, p. 457.
37. Ripert, *op cit*. p. 390.

Validity of exclusion and limitation clauses

UK, US and French case law accepts the principle of the validity of exclusion and limitation clauses. The only difference lies in the assessment of how they are implemented:

Position in UK law

This matter is governed under UK law by the Unfair Contract Terms Act 1977. Section 2 (1) provides that 'A person cannot by reference to any contract term or to a notice given to persons generally or to particular persons exclude or restrict his liability for death or personal injury resulting from negligence'.

The term "negligence" embraces both the tort of negligence and the breach of any contractual obligation to exercise reasonable skill or care (s 1 (1)).

In the case of other loss or damage, a person can exclude or restrict his liability for negligence if the term or notice satisfies the requirement of reasonableness.[38]

So far, UK courts have not had to hand down decisions on the validity of exclusion or limitation clauses issued by classification societies. Some decisions have been reached, however, on onshore disputes, showing that 'such a clause operates as a warning and may prevent the plaintiff from establishing breach of the duty to exercise reasonable care and skill or reliance on the report in relation to inaccurate or uninspected part'.

Some authors consider that much will depend upon the proper construction of the clause.[39]

Position in US law

Exclusion clauses in maritime contracts in the USA are not against public policy and will be upheld. As one court stated:

> It should be a basic policy of the law to hold parties to the contracts they make. The business and industry of the country function because contracts are binding and enforced by the courts. It is only when there is some overriding reason for public concern, some real and valid problem, that a party should be allowed to evade the terms of a contract he has agreed to.[40]

Certain conditions, however, determine their acceptability to a judge[41]:

- — Parties should have relatively equal bargaining power;
- — Protection afforded by exclusion clauses should extend only to ordinary negligence, not gross negligence;
- — They are strictly construed in case of ambiguity.

38. R. Lawson: *Exclusion clauses* (Oyez Longman, London 1983), p. 129.
39. Jackson and Powell, *op. cit.* p. 96.
40. *Hudson Waterways Corp*, 436 F Supp at 605, 1978, AMC at 350–351.
41. H. M. McCormack: 'Warranties and disclaimers', [1988] *Tulane Law Review*, **62**, pp. 552–560.

As regards the validity of exclusion or limitation clauses stipulated by classification societies, court decisions are not always in concordance:

— In *The Tradeways II* case, the court held the clause invalid on the grounds of public policy.

— In *The Gulf Tampa Drydock* case,[42] the Fifth Circuit directed the District Court to consider its effect, if any, upon remand suggesting at least the possibility that the disclaimer clause was enforceable. The Lower Court, after it had reconsidered the case and the directives given to it by the Court of Appeals, finally held the clause to be 'overbroad and unenforceable as contrary to public policy'.

— In *The Amoco Cadiz* case,[43] the court, while expressing 'some doubt whether the broad exculpatory clause contained within the certificates issued by ABS is legally enforceable', nevertheless relied on the clause as evidence that the classification society had not assumed a contractual obligation to indemnify its client.

Some authors think that exclusion clauses will continue to influence the outcome of adjudication, despite the varying weight courts have accorded to these provisions.[44]

Position in French law

The validity of exclusion or limitation clauses inserted in the general conditions of service of classification societies has been in no doubt in French law, since the famous decision of 15 May 1923 by the Supreme Court of Appeals in *The Armor* case.[45] By applying to classification societies the solutions previously adopted for information agencies, the court drew a distinction between gross negligence and ordinary negligence with only the latter being subject to a disclaimer by non-liability clauses. Since that date, the Supreme Court of Appeals has constantly maintained its attitude, considering that only wilful misrepresentation or proven gross default could stand in the way of the will of the parties. It is precisely the freedom of agreements, and in particular article 1134 of the Civil Code, that provides a basis for this precedent.[46] Such contracts must be performed in good faith: if there is wilful misrepresentation, and gross default presumes this, the debtor has acted in bad faith and the contract can no longer protect him. This solution, in conformity with commercial law on land,[47] is at present increasingly

42. *Gulf Tampa Drydock Co* v. *Germanischer Lloyd*, US Court of Appeals, 5th Circuit, 20 January 1981, in Federal Reporter, 2nd series, 874 and US District Court, Tampa Division, 18 June 1981.
43. Cf *supra* at note 18, 1986, AMC at 1952.
44. J. D. Gordan: 'The liability of marine surveyors and ship classification societies', *Journal of Maritime Law & Commerce*, **18**, No. 2, April 1988, p. 306.
45. Cass Req. 15 May 1923, Dalloz 1923–1–15.
46. Article 1134: 'Les conventions légalement formées tiennent lieu de loi à ceux qui les ont faites.'
47. Cour de Cassation, Com., 15 June 1959, Dalloz 1960, p. 17, note A. Rodière.

asserted.[48] And yet this does not prevent a few decisions going against the general tendency.[49]

CLASSIFICATION SOCIETY OBLIGATIONS TO THIRD PARTIES

A preliminary remark on terminology is required with regard to 'third parties' or 'penitus extranei'. They constitute all those who, while not being bound by the requirements of the contract and rules of classification societies, are nevertheless concerned by their operations.

They are many in number:

— Professionals who obtain information from classification societies' registers.
— Hull insurers using the class reference of a given vessel to calculate the premium to be charged to the owner.
— The purchaser in the sale of a ship, who frequently takes account of notations on the classification certificate. Like the insurer, he may be led into error, not only by omissions, but also by the assignment of a mark proved inappropriate by experience.
— Carriers and charterers, and cargo insurers, who often take account of such information in assessing the risks of maritime transport.

After a shipping accident, the classification society, through its function in promoting ship safety, is often in the front line becoming the target for those whose interests have been harmed by the event including: the crew; the owner of the ship; families of the victims of a shipwreck; public authorities whose shoreline has been polluted by oil spills; seamen's unions; conservation and protection associations. This is not an exhaustive list, and it would be hopeless to try and list all the potential third parties concerned, remotely or closely, with ship safety.

The obligations of classification societies towards such third parties raise the largest number of problems, and are some of the most difficult to solve. They are behind three quarters of the disputes that have arisen over the last 15 years. Because of the extent of this question, the bases and grounds of such responsibilities will be examined first. The means of protection deployed by societies against such claims will then be considered, as will the extent of their effectiveness.

48. Marseilles Commercial Court, 10 February 1926, DMF 1926, p. 234; Aix Appeal Court, 15 February 1927, DMF, 1927, p. 196; Tunis Appeal Court, 23 February 1955, DMF 1956, p. 87 and Jurisclasseur Périodique 1955, 8310; Cour de Cassation, Com., 15 June 1959, Dalloz 1960, p. 97, note A Rodière; Paris Appeal Court, 12 December 1968, DMF 1969, p. 223; Paris Maritime Arbitration Tribunal, Sentence no. 115, 5 April 1974, DMF 1974, p. 635; Marseilles Commercial Court, 6 January 1978, DMF 1978, p. 310.

49. In this case, the Strasbourg Commercial Court had pronounced null and void a clause exempting Lloyd's Register for any negligence by its agents, without even making the traditional distinction between 'slight' and 'gross' defaults. Strasbourg Commercial Court, 6 February 1963, *Revue Trimestrielle de Droit Commercial* 1963, p. 390, note Mr Govare.

Grounds for the liability of classification societies towards third parties

Three conditions must apply before third party liability is involved: injury, negligence and a causal link between the two. As earlier seen, any negligence arises from failure to comply with a classification contract or rules. With regard to third parties who by definition are not parties to the contract, the fault consists of negligence or imprudence by the classification society.

The principles of tort liability are applied in different ways under the UK, US and French legal systems.

Position in UK law

In UK law, negligence is the commission of an act that a reasonable person would not commit, or the omission to do something that a reasonable person would do with regard to the duty of care each individual has to his neighbour. When a complaint for negligence is filed, the burden of proof is on the plaintiff who has to prove:

- — that the defendant owed the plaintiff a duty of care;
- — that there has been a breach of that duty;
- — that the breach has caused harm to the plaintiff.

On these principles, UK case law has established the foundations of tort liability by professionals towards third parties. This general system of liability will be examined, before the specific case of classification societies is considered.

Professional tort liability towards third parties

Judges have been influenced by two considerations in establishing the rules of professional tort liability[50]: first, the need to protect consumers against certain actions; and secondly, the need not to paralyse certain activities. Several concerns have been taken into account.

To begin with, one has had to admit that many of the activities of a professional are aimed at protecting his client against other individuals with opposing interests. It has also been realised that certain actions, particularly those involving the issue of reports or the publication of information, had such far-reaching repercussions that it was becoming unfair to impose liability on a professional for all the foreseeable consequences of his mistakes.

The tendency of the courts has therefore been to limit those cases to two situations where a professional is generally bound by a duty of care towards third parties:

- — where the professional undertakes to perform work of which the main beneficiary will be a third party;
- — where a professional who publishes a report or issues a certificate knows

50. Jackson and Powell: *op. cit.*, pp. 7 *et seq.*

that his client will use the document in relations with third parties, for the purpose of inducing particular behaviour on his part.

It is against this background that one must see the precedent of *The Morning Watch* case, which for the first time in the UK laid down the tort liability of a classification society with regard to third parties.

The Morning Watch case[51] *and tort liability of classification societies*

The problem raised in this case was as follows: when a classification society surveys a vessel, does it owe a duty of care not to cause pecuniary loss to persons other than the owners, who are liable to rely upon the results of that survey?

The plaintiff, Mariola Marine Corporation, was a US company which had purchased *The Morning Watch*, an 80 foot steel-hulled motor yacht, in March 1985. The yacht had just been surveyed by a Lloyd's Register of Shipping surveyor, and had effectively been given a clean bill of health and classed 100-A1. The plaintiff contended that *The Morning Watch* in fact had serious defects which rendered her unseaworthy and which should have been detected had the survey been properly conducted. Mariola's claim, as pleaded, was for economic loss suffered as a consequence of relying upon allegedly negligent misstatements by the LR surveyor.

Did LR owe Mariola a duty of care? This was the first question asked by Mr Justice Phillips in his judgment in the Queen's Bench Division. His response was that a duty of care will arise only where:

- it is reasonably foreseeable to the defendant that the plaintiff is liable to rely upon his statement;
- there is the necessary proximity between the plaintiff and the defendant;
- it is just and reasonable in all the circumstances to impose a duty of care on the part of the defendant to the plaintiff.

On the first point, the judge found that in the circumstances of this case it was reasonably foreseeable by LR that a purchaser would be influenced by the results of the special survey in considering whether to buy the vessel.

But that was not in itself enough to establish a duty of care in a case of economic loss. There must also be a sufficient degree of proximity between plaintiff and defendant, and there is no universal test to determine whether the necessary proximity exists. Under the LR system of classification, parties other than the owner of the classified vessel were expected to rely on the fact that a vessel was maintained in class as providing an assurance that the vessel was kept in good condition. But the primary purpose of the system was to enhance the safety of life and property at sea, rather than to protect the economic interests of those involved in shipping.

51. *Mariola Marine Corporation* v. *Lloyds Register of Shipping, The 'Morning Watch'* [1990] 1 Lloyd's Rep. 547.

Insofar as negligent classification was liable to harm economic interests, there were no general grounds for distinguishing those of the charterers, the mortgagee or the purchaser, all of whom were at risk from this particular form of economic loss. For these reasons, the judge held that Mariola had failed to establish that LR owed it any duty of care when the special survey was carried out, or the interim certificate issued before the vessel's sale.

As the requisite proximity is not established, the High Court did not answer the question of whether it would be just and reasonable to impose a duty of care, and did not consider the effect of the standard form of limitation clause written on the interim certificate issued by the LR surveyor.

Position in US law

In US law, the Second Restatement of Torts[52] delineates under what circumstances a party may be held liable to third parties for an action it takes, which it should recognise as necessary for the protection of third parties.

Under 324 A, a party is liable to third parties only if its failure to exercise reasonable care increases the risk of harm, if it has undertaken to perform a duty owed by the other party to the third party, or if harm is suffered because the other party or the third party relied upon the undertaking.

How are such provisions interpreted by US courts?

In *The Tradeways II* case, the judge tried to define the two extra-contractual obligations to be observed by the classification society towards its client, and which is also imposed towards third parties:

— The first duty is to survey and class vessels in accordance with rules and standards established and promulgated by the society for that purpose,

— The second duty is that of due care in detection of defects in the ship it surveys and the corollary of notification thereof to the owner and charterer.

The court noted a potentially insuperable bar to any recovery at law for a breach of the first duty, which 'stems from the rule that the owner of a ship has a non-delegable duty to maintain a seaworthy vessel'. As regards the second obligation, it considers that negligence was not proven, because of the fact that the owner was aware of the ship's defects.

In *The Amoco Cadiz* case, application of §324 A of the Second Restatement of Tort was also refused. The failure to detect already existing dangerous conditions cannot be said to increase the risk in any real or logical manner and is an insufficient basis upon which to impose liability for contribution.

The Pensacola case[53] resembles *The Tradeways II* case in every way. This Liberty ship, built in 1945, had undergone special survey in dry dock at New

52. Restatement (Second) of Tort para. 324A. See also W. Prosver and W. Keeton, *The Law of Tort*, 5th ed. 1984.

53. *Steamship Mutual Underwriting Association Ltd* v. *Bureau Veritas*, 1973, AMC 2184.

Orleans, and the various repairs required by the surveyor to maintain class had been carried out. A few days later, while it was on the way to the Caribbean, it was noticed that the transmission shaft tunnel was flooded. The ship was diverted to Miami and examined by the local surveyor, who recommended certain repairs, and added a restrictive notation to the classification certificate. Having resumed its voyage, the *Pensacola* sank in heavy seas a few days later. The P&I Club sued the classification society for negligence committed during the survey by the Miami surveyor, and for failure to comply with the obligation to guarantee the ship's seaworthiness. On the first point, the District Court in Louisiana admitted that certain negligences had been committed in examining the ship, but it was not proven that such negligence was the cause of the accident. On the second point, it repeated, with approval, the argument put forward by the judge in *The Tradeways II* case: it is not possible to apply to a classification society the obligation to guarantee the seaworthiness of a vessel, placed squarely by maritime law on the shipowner.

In the *Shipping Corporation of India* (SCI) case,[54] the classification society was sued by the owner of several ships built and classed in Yugoslavia. The owner, SCI, based its claim both on the contractual and tort basis, and invoked four types of negligence allegedly committed by the classification society.

In its defence, ABS argued that SCI's negligence claim was not cognizable in maritime tort. Its position was based on the Supreme Court's decision in *East River SS Corporation* v. *Transamerica Delaval Inc*,[55] in a marine context, a manufacturer in a commercial relationship has no duty under either a negligence or strict products liability theory to prevent a product from injuring itself'. ABS used also the Fifth Circuit's decision in *Employers Insurance of Wausau*,[56] which extended the ruling in *East River* to hold that it also applied to contracts for professional services rendered in connection with the construction of a product by a party other than the builder. In both cases, the courts based their decisions on the principle that contract law provides adequate remedies in a commercial setting where parties are of equal enough bargaining power to allocate risks of defects among themselves.

The New York Court, following the same line of argument as in the two preceding cases, considered that 'there is no reason to impose an extra-contractual duty on one who contracts to provide professional services in a commercial context' and turned down the SC1 plea.

In the *Continental Insurance Co* case,[57] the dispute concerned water damage to cargo shipped aboard the M/V *American New York* on its maiden voyage. The defendant, Daewo Shipbuilding and Heavy Machinery Ltd (Daewo), builder of

54. *Shipping Corporation of India Ltd* v. *American Bureau of Shipping*, USDC SD New York, 27 July 1990.

55. *East River SS Corp* v. *Transamerica Delaval Inc*, 476 US 858, 106 S.Ct 2295, L.Ed. 2nd 855 (1986).

56. *Employers Insurance of Wausau* v. *Suwanee River Sea Lines Inc*, 866 F. 2d 752 (1989).

57. *Continental Insurance Co* v. *Daewo Shipbuilding & Heavy Machinery Ltd, Daewo Shipbuilding and American Bureau of Shipping*, USDJ New York, 10 July 1988, 86 Civ. 8255 (RLC).

the vessel, contracted with the defendant ABS 'to review specifications for the vessel, survey it and certify its compliance with rules promulgated by this society'. Cargo insurers, who were subrogated to the claims of the cargo owners, alleged that ABS owed users of the vessel a duty to discover the defect which had caused leakage, and had breached that duty. Plaintiffs claimed only that ABS was remiss in not reinspecting the manhole cover on one of the vessel's ballast tanks, which was at the origin of the water damage.

The Court considered that ABS' duty was delimited by its contract with the builder as this contract only involved declaring the conformity of the ship to the classification society rules, and was not an absolute guarantee of its seaworthiness. 'To extend a classification society's duty to the operational details of the vessel's management would both ignore the clear limit of its contractual duty, and make it an absolute insurer of the vessel.'

In this case, plaintiffs failed to come forward with evidence on two essential aspects of the claim: first, that ABS had certified the fitness of the sensing device, in violation of its rules; and second, that ABS certification was the proximate cause of the damage.

Position in French law

In France, articles 1382 *et seq.* of the Civil Code apply, which means that a decision has to be taken as to whether or not the injured third party has suffered harm through the fault of the classification society.

A large number of disputes concern ship sales. The purchaser considers himself entitled to rely on the accuracy of the information published in classification registers. If an error occurs it could lead to certain and direct damage, because the purchaser has negotiated on the basis of his reliance on the class. It remains to be seen whether the fault can be attributed to the classification society.

If the purchaser can establish a deliberate wrong done to him, or a conspiracy with the vendor to defraud him, the society is fully responsible and cannot limit compensation for the damage caused. As regards involuntary faults, responsibility must be assessed in the light of circumstances, particularly any commitments the society has entered into with its client.

It is worth recalling that the rules of tort liability can be set aside, even among persons who are not bound by a contract. This is the famous theory of 'contract groups' developed by the Supreme Court of Appeals in the last 10 years.[58] The latest decision[59] laid down that, in a group of contracts contractual liability necessarily governs action for compensation taken by all those who have suffered injury because they had a link with the initial contract. In this case, stated the court, since the debtor of the obligation should have foreseen the consequences of

58. On the theory of 'contractual groups', see: Cour de Cassation, 9 October 1979, *Bulletin Civil I* no. 241, *Gazette du Palais* 1980-1-249; Cour de Cassation, 29 May 1984, *Dalloz* 1985, 213 and *Gazette du Palais* 1983-2-437; Cour de Cassation, 8 March 1988, *Bulletin Civil* no. 69.

59. Cour de Cassation, 21 June 1988, *Dalloz* 1989, 5.

its failure, in accordance with relevant contractual rules, the victim can only take action of a contractual nature, even in the absence of any contract between them.

This line of argument could apply to classification societies, on the grounds that the contracts they have signed with the shipowner or shipyard and subcontractors form a 'contract group' which must be taken into account in assessing their obligations to third parties. An illustration of this is provided by the decisions handed down in *The Cap de la Hague* case.[60] All of them take into account the commitments entered into by the classification society towards the owner, in assessing the seriousness of the faults committed. In fact, the BV remit had been to 'provide technical services on the owner's behalf'. It was not a standard classification contract, since the services in question consisted of stability tests on the dredger *Cap de la Hague*.

In a decision issued on 6 July 1978, the Appeal Court in Douai considered that the classification society had committed imprudences which were at the origin of the shipwreck. It concluded that BV was under an obligation to act for the shipowner in all operations within its attributions, and beyond the competence of the owner, and in particular to verify and adjust operating conditions for the dredger. Setting aside the criticisms formerly expressed in such exceptional criminal case, it should be noted that, in the absence of a formal contract stipulating the extent of the classification society's remit, the judges formed an extensive concept of its obligations, in laying upon it an almost comprehensive and systematic advisory obligation towards its client, and towards third parties.[61]

Protection for classification societies against third parties

Classification societies have tried to restrict the increasingly frequent lawsuits by third parties against their operations. Most such initiatives result from contractual mechanisms. In certain cases, their task is facilitated by the provisions of international maritime conventions.

Legal protection by channelising

No one can protect a defendant by removing the right to take legal action from the victim who was not party to the contract. A legislative intervention is needed. This result is occasionally obtained by the technique of 'channelising', which consists of concentrating the whole of an industrial risk on a single person, presumed to be most appropriate to bear it. This involves two steps: first, a person is designated as liable for damage resulting from the incriminated activity;

60. Douai Appeal Court, 6 July 1978, DMF 1981, p. 153; Cour de Cassation, Criminal Ct, 30 May 1980, DMF 1981, p. 146.

61. *Ibid*. pp. 144–5.

secondly, claims against other persons are prohibited. Such a system has been set up on an international scale for nuclear accidents and damage caused by oil pollution.

Nuclear damage

Such damage is in general unlikely to involve the liability of a classification society, since it comes under the terms of special conventions, which exclude any other liability than that of the nuclear plant operator. Article 11.2 of the Brussels Convention of 25 May 1962 on nuclear merchant ships expressly provides for channelising of liability. A similar provision applies to transportation of radioactive substances by sea, making the operator of the nuclear installation responsible for any damage connected with the special properties of the products being carried.[62]

Oil pollution

The 1984 protocol, amending the Brussels Convention on third party liability for oil pollution damage of 29 November 1969, has effected a considerable improvement in channelising mechanisms. A list of persons against whom 'no claims for compensation damage under this convention or otherwise may be made' is henceforth provided for in art. III, para. 4.

Such persons include: '(b) the pilot or any other person who, without being a member of the crew, performs services for the ship.' This text clearly includes classification societies.

There should be no illusions, however, about the protection offered by channelising. For the moment, it remains uncertain, assuming not only that a convention makes such provision, but also that it has been ratified by the state within which the legal action might be taken.

Legal protection relating to maritime claims

The London Convention of 19 November 1976 on limitation of maritime claims can offer other legal protection to classification societies. The benefit of the limitation of compensation which it involves is no longer attached to a person owning the ship or other, as in the 1957 Convention, but to a claim, which must be maritime, in other words, connected with the operation of the vessel.

62. Sea transport of radioactive substances is governed by the Brussels Convention of 17 December 1971.

Article 1, para. 4 states that 'if any claims set out in Article 2 are made against any person for whose act, neglect or default the shipowner or salvor is responsible, such person shall be entitled to avail himself of the limitation of liability provided for in this Convention'.

Like any other purveyor of services, a classification society could, through an error or negligence, call the shipowner's liability into play. It accordingly comes within the field of application of the London Convention, even though its case has not been specifically included. It must therefore be admitted to avail itself of the limitation provided for in this Convention, provided that the claim made against it is one of those referred to in art. 2. The wording is broad: it enumerates, in the UK and US way, all claims likely to arise during operation of the ship, and in particular: '(a) claims in respect of loss of life or personal injury or loss of or damage to property occurring on board or in direct connection with the operation of the shipowner with salvage operations, and consequential loss resulting therefrom.'

The London Convention, however, remains an instrument of international law, presenting the same drawbacks as those already mentioned if states fail to ratify them or fail to implement their provisions on an international basis.

Contractual protections

Such protections, which result from contractual mechanisms, can be divided into two categories:

- certain classification societies have imposed a 'hold harmless' clause in their contract, under the terms of which the client is responsible for repairing damage not caused solely by the society's negligence;
- others place a warning notice on all documents likely to be used by third parties, namely classification certificates, registers and rules.

What legal value do such provisions have in the various legal systems?

In UK law, the enforceability of exclusionary clauses aimed at third parties will hinge on the extent to which such clauses have been brought to the attention of third parties and the reasonableness of such clauses in the context of the UK. Unfair Contract Terms Act 1977.

French law remains more complex: it considers that third party non-liability clauses can act as warnings. The classification society acts in good faith in supplying information and delivering an opinion based on the widest possible guarantees with which it can surround itself. Such behaviour is legal, and third parties are warned that they cannot reasonably demand absolute certainty in documents available to them. This means that a suit founded by art. 1982 of the Civil Code would have no chance of success against the society, unless the third party could prove, in addition to the injury suffered, an intentional default, a deliberate mistake, equivalent to wilful misrepresentation,[63] or an especially serious default.[64]

CONCLUSION

This investigation of the liability of classification societies, as revealed by French, UK and US case law, has revealed several points.

To begin with, judges display noteworthy caution and, unlike certain press media, do not hold classification societies responsible for all the shortcomings of the maritime safety system. In nearly all examples of case law, the society's liability is assessed in relation to the obligations stipulated in the contract or classification rules, and this situation is taken into account in any relations between the society and any third parties. Even though the matter is eminently technical, judges, with the help of legal experts, make a clear distinction among the various types of contracts and certificates. Cases of negligence are increasingly being examined *in concreto*, in other words in relation to particular circumstances, not with reference to an idealised hyper-competent surveyor, but in relation to the experience of an ordinary, normally skilled and informed surveyor.

Judges also make a very strict examination of how the liability of classification societies is implemented. It is not enough to prove the surveyor's negligence or the injury suffered: the causal link between the two must be demonstrated. Such a link often remains hard to prove, which explains why most legal decisions are given in favour of classification societies.

Numerous decisions highlight the special features of classification societies. They are not like other purveyors of services in the maritime sector. Unlike the shipping authorities, they have no means of coercion concerning faulty vessels: they can merely observe and report, and their report on the condition of the ship is no more than an expression of its conformity to the classification rules they themselves have issued. This represents a fundamental difference between the classification society surveyor and other maritime surveyors. The report provides no sort of 'blessing' on the seaworthiness of the ship, nor on its general level of safety. Safety must be examined against other factors, such as the ability of the crew, or the operating conditions stipulated by the owner.

Finally, despite increasingly frequent legal claims against classification societies, the major balances established over several centuries by maritime law have not been overthrown. The shipyard cannot abrogate its liabilities to the classification society, and remains responsible for latent defects predating delivery of the ship. The same applies to the shipowner who cannot delegate his duty to keep his ship seaworthy because the classification society does not act as

63. Paris, 30 March 1928, Dor Sup. 11, 465; Paris, 12 December 1968, DMF 1969, 223; Tunis, 23 February 1955, JCP 55 II 8809.

64. Strasbourg Commercial Court, 6 February 1963; cf *supra* at note 49.

an insurer, whose function it is to pay out the value of damaged property after an accident. The society's role is in fact to warn of such risks, not to guarantee the absolute safety of every ship it surveys and classes.

It would not be wise judicial policy to alter this fundamental balance, since it would result, either in the disappearance of classification societies, or at any rate in weakening them, to the great detriment of safety on all the seas.

PHILIPPE BOISSON

CHAPTER 2

PRACTICAL AND POLITICAL CONSIDERATIONS

Ship classification is an activity that is central to the whole subject of ship safety but whose terms of reference and parameters are often misunderstood. No observer, however casual, of the shipping scene over the course of the past 12 months or so will fail to have been struck by a marked increase in public and political concern about questions of safety, casualties, and pollution and by the shipping industry's response to these issues.

The *Exxon Valdez* incident has sparked off demands in the USA for double-hulled tankers, demands whose ramifications have still not been finally assessed. The shipping industry still has to consider whether or not this development will fulfil the claims made regarding protection against pollution or whether acceptable equivalents to double-hulled tankers can be found. The exceptionally high losses of bulk carriers in 1990 prompted Lloyd's Register to take the lead in investigating the matter. This resulted in LR's recommendation relating to better control of loading and unloading operations; greater awareness of the sensitivity of the side shell structure in the cargo holds, both to mechanical damage sustained during loading and unloading and to localised corrosion following the carriage of certain cargoes; and immediate repairs to any such defects in the side shell. LR's action was followed by ABS and IACS.

Other incidents include the *Scandinavian Star* tragedy which has led the Norwegian Government to take various domestic and international initiatives; while in the offshore sector, the Cullen report into the *Piper Alpha* disaster will have a major impact on future North Sea safety requirements and procedures. The Secretary General of IMO has voiced increasing concern about the general level of marine safety and every added casualty highlights the inadequacies of the present legislation.

These incidents will result in new recommendations from the IMO in due course, but they will probably take several years to be accepted generally. Meanwhile, the major classification societies and other responsible organisations will be looking into practical ways of reducing risk. For example, the installation of stress monitors on bulk carriers would help to inform the master of any advisable changes of speed or heading in heavy weather.

However, despite these concerns, it is reassuring to note that every dispassionate analysis of global marine casualty statistics (excluding war losses) shows that, while in recent decades public expectation of safety has increased, the casualty rates as a simple percentage of the world fleet have steadily decreased.

Of course this is not to say that claims on underwriters in financial terms have decreased because, in general, ships have become more sophisticated and costly, and repair prices have increased in real terms over the years. Moreover, because the average age of the fleet has increased during the last 10 years, a higher percentage of ships which sustain damage are now declared constructive total losses because of the high cost of repairs *vis-à-vis* their value.

Inevitably, in the wake of a disaster, there are calls for 'absolute' safety standards, regardless of cost or practicability. In hindsight it can seem that regulations are too onerous the day before an accident and too lax the day after it and as Dr Johnson said, 'He who vilifies established authority is sure of an audience.' Such calls for absolute safety are understandable, even if they are known to be unrealistic. But before dismissing them, it is important to establish just what an acceptable standard of safety is.

SAFETY JUDGMENT IN THE MARINE FIELD

There are four main factors to consider in the safety equation: the perceived or calculated risks; technical skill and experience; pressures for cost-effectiveness; and public/political opinion.

The determination of an acceptable standard of safety is a judgment of the relative weight of these factors—a compromise, in other words. The weight given to each component will vary. For example, the pressure for double-hulled tankers in the USA gives added weight to the 'public/political opinion' factor. But I believe these factors are relevant both to the design, construction and maintenance of ships and to their manning and operating requirements.

Largely due to the complex nature of each of the four factors, there is no single body which posseses in sufficient depth the technical, commercial, analytical and political skills to make the major marine safety judgments by itself and has the resources, organisation and authority to apply them consistently throughout the world. This is true of design, construction and maintenance, even more so if operational aspects are also taken into account.

THE ROLE OF INTERNATIONAL CLASSIFICATION SOCIETIES

So where does classification fit in? First, classification societies do not deal with all aspects of safety or seaworthiness. For example, a ship with defective lifeboats or a wrongly loaded ship or an inadequately crewed ship is unseaworthy and may become a casualty, but the classification certificate does not encompass these aspects.

In general, classification societies exist to lay down and update regularly standards of safety in terms of hull structure and essential machinery, and to implement these standards consistently and without prejudice worldwide. The standards for other physical aspects of ship safety such as flotational stability, loadline, safety equipment and radiotelegraphy have been laid down in detail by international convention. The great majority of flag states delegate the implementation of these standards to the major classification societies because the latter are, for the most part, uniquely equipped to deal effectively with them throughout the world.

With this statutory work carried out on behalf of a flag state, a classification society must ensure that country's requirements, in terms of international conventions, are fully met. The society is limited in its authority to implement only the conventions that each country has adopted.

Other aspects of safety, such as determining crewing levels and crew competence remain with the flag states and are not delegated.

When it comes to classification requirements, the society's own rules are used. The knowledge that a ship is designed, built and maintained in accordance with the rules of a major classification society should give the owner and the shipping community confidence that it meets proper standards of quality, safety and reliability in all matters affecting class. The principal concern of classification is safety: this is the core to so many transactions in the shipping industry: for example, insurance, sale and purchase, chartering and finance.

Classification requires integrity, a relationship of honesty and mutual trust between owner, classification society and maritime authority. It also calls for a high level of competence on all sides. This traditional relationship has been put to the test in recent years with changes in the nature of the international shipping industry. There has been a steep decline in the fleets and seafarers of most traditional maritime nations with a rise in new registers; a shedding of traditional responsibilities by shipowners in favour of sub-contracted agencies; poor freight rates; and a growth in new, 'national' classification societies.

How have the classification societies fulfilled their obligation to apply their class rules and statutory requirements consistently in this new climate? Certainly their responsibilities are now greater then ever before. As technical considerations become more complex, and fewer and fewer shipowners maintain an extensive technical capability, the importance of the service provided by the major societies is increased.

Here it is important to differentiate between the majority of classification societies, which quite clearly do not have the capacity to undertake the proper responsibilities of classification, with the major ones which do.

There are a number of reasons why a country might want its own national classification society—from a desire to train its engineers to a matter of national pride. However, the fact is that the vast majority of these societies have no depth or breadth of worldwide coverage and lack the knowledge and expertise they need for this international industry.

WHAT CLASSIFICATION SOCIETIES NEED FOR SUCCESS

By their coverage, advanced data processing, elaborate communications networks and full involvement in all matters concerning the construction of ships and the ways of maintaining their structures and engineering systems, the major societies provide a unique clearing system with technical knowledge and experience. The knowledge and experience of the major societies enable them, through IACS, to provide information to the IMO in the technical preparation of draft safety regulations which, together with classification rules, provide the basis of flag state legislation for safety at sea. Few flag states are organised to carry out statutory surveys other than in their own country and the delegation of this work to classification societies is cheaper than sending their own surveyors around the world whilst also encouraging the harmonisation of classification and statutory survey schedules. Thus the major societies are able to provide a high degree of worldwide consistency—which is as important as it is difficult to achieve.

However sound its rules, a classification society stands or falls by the experience, skill and integrity of those who apply them. Therefore it is essential to choose the right people to become surveyors. Only by ensuring that they have the necessary skills and technical information, and by giving them proper support wherever they are in the world is it possible to achieve consistency on a worldwide basis. All these factors point to the need for classification societies to employ exclusive surveyors who work solely to their standards.

At LR we currently employ 1,740 technical staff, of whom 1,690 are graduates, the rest being mature chartered engineers or technicians. Of the graduates, 1,675 have engineering degrees and the others have degrees in mathematics or science. These are all people employed exclusively by us and who work to our standards; and they are supported by approximately 1,780 administrative staff. Our staff operate out of more than 245 offices around the world and serve more than 100 countries.

It is important that staff stay abreast of changes and advances in technology. To that end, LR has recently become committed to: a graduate training scheme; an induction course for new mature entrants; a comprehensive range of obligatory courses on specific technical subjects for surveyors at appropriate stages of career development; 'on the job' training under the control of senior staff throughout the world; and a revised management training development scheme. The quality of work within LR's Ship Division throughout the world is now audited against international standards of management and any irregularities indicating a lack of specific training is subject to immediate remedial action.

On the same basis, members of the IACS have recently decided that, as a condition of future membership, each society must implement within its own organisation a quality system complying with ISO9001 requirements to ensure consistent application of standards and must submit the system to external audit. The IS09001 standard for quality management systems encompasses the function of managing technical design standards, and each member of the IACS must

Plate 1. A defective hydrant on the fire main. The only way to close the hydrant is by means of a wooden plug rounded with tarpaulin and held to the hydrant and fire main by rope. Water is pouring out in all directions. (Lack of compliance with SOLAS, Chapter II — 2, regulation 4/1 and 6.1.)
[See page 39]

Plate 2. A fire hose with one coupling missing rendering it unusable for fighting purposes. In addition the fire nozzle is not of an approved dual-purpose type incorporating a shutoff. (Lack of compliance, Chapter II — 2, regulation 4/7.1 and 8.4.)

Plate 3. A securing ring on the hatch coaming for deck cargoes, containers or the like. The welded pat eye is eaten away by corrosion, as is basically the entire hatch coaming system.

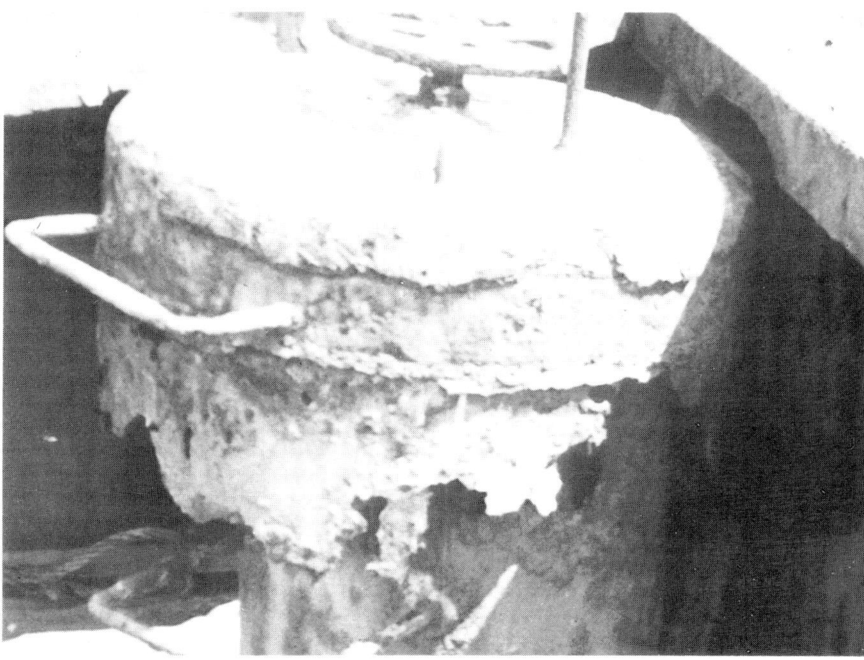

Plate 4. A corroded ventilation duct for special category space, this part almost completely eaten away by corrosion. (Lack of compliance with SOLAS II — 2, regulation 16 3/9.)

Plate 5. The outer shell plating seriously indented over eight frames. In addition, heavy pitting is noted in the entire plate.

Plate 6. A close-up of the pittings in Plate 5. The depth of the pittings can be determined by looking at the shadows cast. It is suggested that more than 55 per cent of the material is corroded away.

demonstrate an adequate capacity to develop and update regularly classification rules. Clearly it is vital that these external audits are carried out effectively, without fear or favour or political intervention.

Approval to ISO9001 is an increasingly valuable asset to the industry as it represents regulation by independent and agreed international standards.

This is an area in which LR has particular expertise which is through its subsidiary company LRQA Ltd, which is the first certification body in the UK to gain accreditation through the National Accreditation Council for Certification Bodies, the first such organisation to be granted accreditation by the Dutch government, and a leading player in the international quality field. Since being set up with an independent board in 1985 LRQA has certified 3,000 groups, trade associations or companies. LRQA's experience extends well beyond the inspection of manufacturing companies' systems: some 20 per cent of its work has been in service industries. It is this capability that has enabled it to offer quality management systems assessments and quantitative risk assessment techniques for the maritime industry.

It is now generally accepted that 80 per cent of maritime disasters are caused by human error. Taken with formal risk and consequence assessment techniques that have been applied increasingly to maritime problems over the past 20 years, the quality/safety management approach is one that will significantly help to reduce this factor. Managers must continue to be responsible for what they do, but the formalisation of good management practice can only be beneficial. Those who carry responsibility for the safety of life, the environment and property must never be satisfied and all possible improvements must constantly be pursued.

RESEARCH AND RULE DEVELOPMENT

LR uses adverse service feedback to prompt changes in its rules and has a fast and positive mechanism for doing this: the research in bulk carrier losses cited earlier is an example of this approach.

Research is also a product of new technical developments: a ship cannot be classed unless published classification rules exist and have been complied with. The competent classification societies are approached by the builder or designer of new technology ships to discuss new design criteria and new design configuration and, if necessary, accelerated research programmes are initiated by these societies.

Before such a new design of ship is classed by one of the major classification societies, rules generally have to be developed, published and circulated worldwide to the Technical Committee members for comment, amended as necessary, formally approved by the Technical Committee (which meets twice a year) and published. Normally this process is completed in well under a year. It is hard to conceive of a more effective process for the promotion of fast and safe technical advance by the combination of innovative design with extensive practical experience.

There is certainly no room for complacency—but classification societies are not likely to run that risk since they are, by their nature, always in the hot seat.

The interests of owners, builders, flag states and underwriters are often opposed to each other, while the interests of the seafarers themselves and the general public must be taken into consideration.

The major classification societies have grown up in the centre of this conflict of interests, and if they had not continually demonstrated their ability to resolve such conflicts with impartiality, integrity and technical skill they would not have remained in existence.

The first classification society, LR, originated in 1760 in response to the needs of underwriters. A conflict of interest developed between owners and underwriters, and LR was reconstituted in 1834 with a permanent committee consisting of equal numbers of merchants, owners and underwriters. Since that time, no single interest has predominated—a principle underlined by the constitution of LR's Classing Committee. This committee, unique to LR, is made up of London-based shipowners, underwriters and P&I club managers, who serve on a rota basis. It meets at LR's headquarters each week to confirm the classification of new ships, to determine whether class is suspended or withdrawn and, more importantly, to act as the final arbiter on difficult cases relating to the class of existing ships. The particular value of this process is that shipowners and insurance interests have equal representation and debate such problematic cases to an agreed conclusion.

THE PROBLEMS CLASSIFICATION SOCIETIES FACE

Of course conflicts of interest and issues of safety sometimes come to a head and become matters for the courts.

Classification societies, like other professional bodies, view with apprehension the danger of legal liabilities escalating out of all proportion. Judgments of safety levels are subjective matters and can often be disputed: courts seem often tempted to examine such judgments against a standard of absolute safety and with the benefit of hindsight.

If this tendency is not resisted, professional bodies will be put into an impossible position: they may continue to make honest judgments against the prospect of a level of damages which it is impossible to meet and which may become uninsurable, or technical judgments may be made on the most conservative possible basis (which will unduly increase the economic burden on the shipping industry), or technical judgments may be hedged to a point where they become valueless.

It is difficult to make this point with any force without appearing to be asking for immunity from responsibility for error or incompetence. Nevertheless, the international classification societies face a real threat and it would be wrong not to recognise it.

This challenge can only be met by acting with integrity, by taking every possible step to make the service as efficient as possible and by trying to make sure that performance is not judged against a standard of absolute safety applied by infallible people in ideal circumstances. However, some owners do put pressure on classification societies to compromise proper standards and under the threat of losing their business to some more compliant society some societies do succumb to such pressure.

IS THERE AN ALTERNATIVE?

If a real conflict of interest can arise in this way, is there some other contractual system that will provide the same benefits without this potential disadvantage?

Amongst the proposed solutions put forward at different times by different interest groups are: the creation of a new, single world classification society; the abolition of the existing system, and the creation of another, more closely linked with the underwriters; and the nationalisation of classification societies.

Taking the concept of a single classification society first—this ignores some essential points: theoretically, it may be possible for the technical capacity of the major societies to be reproduced in a single body, but this would be a considerable undertaking, requiring the total harmonisation of rules in all their diversity, an integration of colossal computer facilities and a single survey force both centrally and in ports and shipyards. Such a force would not be highly motivated to make technical decisions with a sensible regard for economic viability or urgency.

On a personal level, the motivation and personal pride which sustains individual surveyors in the face of all kinds of pressure—not to mention the inherent difficulties of their job—could hardly be built up and maintained within such a body.

Even if such a single society were to be formed, it is unlikely that it would be able to survive, as it would be difficult to see how it would be funded. Since classification is not a profitable business by normal commercial criteria, the lack of any contribution from the new classification activities might well prove very limiting.

What about the insurance market, which should have a vested interest in safety? One of the problems here is that underwriters are understandably reluctant to become deeply involved in technical matters. If classification societies were primarily responsible to underwriters, then underwriters would have to develop a very extensive technical as well as administrative capacity. Given the structure of the international insurance markets it would be difficult to establish a single executive body, or a cooperative of national markets responsible for directing and taking central responsibility for the way in which the world's classification services are provided, regulated and paid for.

Individual underwriters often explain their inability to take effective combined action in support of proper standards by referring to the competitive nature of their own market, especially in a time of over-capacity. It is not easy to see how this could be reconciled with the motivation and impartiality needed for central control of classification.

The third suggestion, namely that the responsibilities of the classification societies should be assumed by the governments of the countries in which they are based, is often proposed as the panacea that will resolve all conflicting interests. However, this turns out to be no more realistic than the others. Some states, including a number where a substantial proportion of the world's fleet is registered, have demonstrated a greater concern for the registration revenue than for the maintenance of proper standards. The slow progress of port state control also shows how many governments are reluctant to make and enforce safety judgments in this area. The business of safety is hardly a remunerative one.

Classification is fundamentally an international service requiring world coverage and independence from a particular national interest.

It is far from certain that all the flag states would be able and willing to expand their technical and administrative skills to the point necessary to support this organisational function, let alone fulfil their obligation to monitor the effectiveness of those societies to which they delegate work.

The notion of transferring responsibility for classification to national authorities in preference to the present framework does not, of course, address what would happen in those countries, which had no society to nationalise. Further, responsible governments are unable to prevent their owners flagging out to less responsible ones and this is cause for real concern.

It is disturbing to note that, despite the increase in importance of public and political opinion in the safety equation, the political will to maintain standards seems, in world terms, to be getting weaker rather than stronger. This appears to be largely due to the almost unrestricted freedom to break the natural line of political authority by flagging out. This weakening is all the more significant if it is correct to suggest that the ultimate authority in the judgment and application of safety levels, whether at national or international level, must be a political authority.

An acceptable level of safety can only be set, maintained and applied worldwide by the close co-operation of a number of groups in the integrated structure. This means it is vital that each of these groups is itself subject to the disciplined application of proper standards and is able to speak with a single voice when it is necessary to do so.

Port state control is an area which should be strengthened, and which should be carried out uniformly, without fear or favour or political intervention. The operation of substandard ships is a global concern, but at present the European 'Paris Memorandum' states are, with the US Coast Guard, making a more throroughgoing job of port state control than others in the world. If governments were to be more selective, if port state control and similar checks were to be enforced, if underwriters were able to distinguish effectively between good and bad performance, and if classification societies were to realise that by openly succumbing to commercial pressure other societies would be preferred to them, proper standards would be maintained.

There will continue to be an entirely understandable public yearning for a simple, cheap and independent method of maintaining world safety standards at an acceptable level, but finding a practical solution is a little harder.

JOHN B. HUTCHISON

CHAPTER 3

THE UNDERWRITERS' PERSPECTIVE

THE ROLE OF CLASSIFICATION SOCIETIES

To understand the role of the classification societies, in particular why they have developed to their current status, it is necessary to examine the rules of the classification societies.

Classification

Nowadays, public attention is focused on environmental problems following casualties with tankers, particularly tankers carrying persistent oil. However, almost all these types of casualties are caused by negligence of the crew and while such casualties may be avoided by training the crew and by adopting stricter rules in this area, the problems addressed in this chapter relate solely to matters regarding the general condition of the ships.

Going back in history, the first registers were established over 200 years ago. Their purpose was to provide a reliable source for underwriters who could then record matters relating to the individual ships of interest to them. From the underwriters' point of view, the object today is exactly the same. However, it is not only underwriters who now rely on the classification societies. National authorities also rely on classification societies to ensure that certain standards are complied with in order to safeguard life and property at sea and to avoid the environmental problems following casualties—in particular tanker casualties, and casualties with ships carrying highly poisonous chemicals.

Although classification societies' supervision of design and arrangement of a structure of new buildings is rarely criticised, underwriters, charterers and cargo owners alike have, in recent years, raised much criticism of the way in which the classification societies deal with matters in relation to ships in operation.

Classification in the operational phase

Compliance with the classification rule requirements in the operational phase is verified by the society through a system of periodic surveys. The most comprehensive of these surveys takes place every five years. In the interim period various parts of the ship undergo annual surveys, depending on the class to which the vessel is assigned.

However, the classification society does not, of course, follow the ship all the time. Therefore it is the owners' duty, in the first instance, to act in accordance with the rules in order to maintain a valid class. The owner is also obliged to maintain the ship to the standard rules at all times and to furnish the classification societies with all information that may influence its decisions in connection with that classification.

Periodic surveys

The classification societies have detailed rules for the annual surveys, intermediate surveys, renewal surveys and other periodic surveys. These rules set out time limits within which these surveys must be carried out, but there is also a rule concerning the postponement of periodic surveys. According to the rules, classification societies may postpone periodic surveys upon consideration of each separate case, and the phrasing of the rules does not give a definite time limit within which the periodic surveys shall take place.

Retention of class

In order to retain the class, the owners are, amongst other things, obliged to inform the classification society without delay if the hull or other items on board covered by classification sustain a certain amount of damage. If this damage is of such an extent that it may be presumed to lead to a condition of class requirement by the classification society then the vessel is to be surveyed at the first port of call or subject to further instructions from the classification society. The survey should then be conducted to the extent considered necessary by the surveyor.

When repairs to the hull or other items covered by classification are considered to be of any significance, the work is to be carried out under the supervision of a surveyor appointed by the classification society.

Withdrawal of class

The classification society may withdraw a vessel's class where the assumption regarding the maintenance and handling of the vessel or the provision for retention of class have been breached. Withdrawal of class may take effect immediately or after a specified period of time. According to the rules, withdrawal may also be made on the condition that it will only come into effect if the owners have rectified the problems leading to the withdrawal within a stipulated time.

TODAY'S EXPERIENCE

There have been a number of tragic losses of bulk carriers—12 were lost in 1991 and seven so far in 1992. There have also been a number of passenger ships lost, the latest one being the *Oceanos* which was lost off the South African coast following a reported explosion in the engine room.

Instead of trying to explain today's experience with fully classed vessels, the plates appearing opposite page 42 demonstrate the experience of Assuranceforeningen Skuld with fully classed vessels. Although these vessels were all fully classed, they were not accepted for entry with Assuranceforeningen Skuld.

Plate 1 shows a defective hydrant on the fire main. The only way to close the hydrant is by means of a wooden plug rounded with tarpaulin and held to the hydrant and fire main by rope. Water is pouring out in all directions. (Lack of compliance with SOLAS, Chapter II–2 regulation 4/1 and 6.1.) In plate 2 a fire hose is shown with one coupling missing rendering if unusable for fighting purposes. In addition the fire nozzle is not of an approved dual-purpose type incorporating a shutoff. (Lack of compliance, Chapter II–2 regulation 4/7.1 and 8.4.) A securing ring on the hatch coaming for deck cargoes, containers or the like is shown in plate 3. The welded pat eye is eaten away by corrosion, as is basically the entire hatch coaming system. In plate 4 there is a corroded ventilation duct for special category space, this part almost completely eaten away by corrosion. (Lack of compliance with SOLAS II–2 regulation 16 3/9.)

Details of the vessel shown in plates 5 and 6 are as follows. The vessel was built in Japan 1973. It has a gross tonnage of slightly more than 9,000 tons and is classed by one of the recognised classification societies. The last annual survey of the vessel took place in July 1990, where the load-line certificate was also renewed as was the safety construction certificate and the safety equipment certificate.

The inspection in November 1990, during which these photographs were taken was slightly more than four months after the issuance of the certificates referred to.

In plate 5 the outer shell plating is seriously indented over eight frames and, in addition, heavy pitting is noted in the entire plate. Plate 6 shows a close-up from the pittings above. The depths of the pittings can be determined by looking at the shadows cast. It is suggested that more than 55 per cent of the material is corroded away.

When the surveyor made his inspection, he found a telegram sent by the master to the owners of the following wording.

TOP/URGENT SHIP/CRACK TEMPORARY ARRESTED N/AFRAID THINNESS OFSHPLATE AT/CRACK N/CEMENT BOX/MAYNOT HOLD/IF BAD

WEATHER OUTSIDE ALSO/IF LEAK/AGAIN AFRAID NOT ABLE/CONTAIN/ WATER DUE PUMPS SUSPECT/N MDO/VERY CRITICAL ROB/8MT MINUS UNPUMPABLE/MAY NOT/ENOKGH 4/MANOVER/IF STAY/TTO LOND/ ANDO PLSHELP/DO UTMOST/-SHIP INNERANCHG 4/PERMANENT PAIR N/BUNKERS

MASTER

WHY THIS EXPERIENCE?

The rules of the classification societies and the environment in which they have to work have led to these unfortunate developments. Taking a closer look at the rules and regulations of the classification societies it can be seen that in very important areas regarding the vessel's seaworthiness the general terms are not at all clear. For example:

> If the hull . . . sustains damage of such extent that it *may be presumed* to invalidate the class conditions, the society is to be informed *without delay*.

> Owners are to submit complete and correct information on the vessel and its use which would be of *significance* to the society . . .

> The society may accept to postpone periodical surveys upon consideration in each separate case.

It is appreciated that it is necessary to have rules which are flexible to a certain extent. Unfortunately the flexibility on postponements and the issuance of interim certificates in particular, often result in owners changing from one classification society to another, to avoid carrying out repairs.

But why are the classification societies so willing to shut their eyes and postpone repairs of damage or wear and tear which clearly render the vessel unseaworthy?

Look for example, at LR which is an independent, non-profit making authority, controlled by a committee representing, amongst others, shipowners, shipbuilders and underwriters. As it is a non-profit making organisation one would think LR would act independently in the interests of those relying on the work carried out.

However, even non-profit making organisations have to work in a competitive environment, and classification societies fear that an owner will simply find another classification society which is more receptive to his request for interim certificates and postponements of surveys.

Competition and flexibility are normally good things, but when it comes to such a thing as classification it can be rather dangerous. Who, for example, would like extended flexibility and postponement of repairs with respect to airplanes?

CONSEQUENCES OF THE EXPERIENCE

The consequence of such an experience is that nobody in the industry—be they hull underwriters, P&I underwriters or charterers—relies completely on what the classification societies are doing.

If an owner applies for cover with hull underwriters, they will give a quotation subject to the vessel in question being condition surveyed with the same procedure applying to the P&I clubs. Very often it is difficult to coordinate these surveys. However, with second and third follow-up surveys it is almost always necessary to carry out repairs with the approval of the classification society involved.

Furthermore, if the owners wish to fix the vessel to certain charterers, the charterers will want to approve the vessel and send a surveyor to make a general condition survey.

It is only in recent years that underwriters and charterers have found it necessary to make their own condition surveys. These surveys are made for one reason only—to check that classification societies are abiding by their own rules and withdrawing the vessel's class if there are outstanding repairs affecting its seaworthiness. Withdrawal of class is the only effective means of protecting the underwriters, because withdrawal of class means there is no insurance cover.

Generally speaking, one can hardly see the advantages to the industry as a whole: someone in the industry has to pay for four surveyors instead of just one. Underwriters and charterers are also having to employ staff and spend time on discussing differences in the various surveyors' findings—not a rewarding task as it is such a waste of time and money.

HOW CAN THINGS BE CHANGED?

Basically, things could be changed in one of two ways: one is the 'American way' where classification societies should be held responsible for what they are doing; the second way is an improved cooperation between classification societies who adhere to stricter rules.

If the classification societies were responsible for their work, those doing a poor job would have to pay extremely high insurance premiums and for that reason would have to charge higher fees and no doubt the owners with well maintained ships would leave them. This solution would also be advantageous to the owners, who spend an adequate amount of money on maintenance. They would of course have no objection to the surveys being carried out in a proper way.

The disadvantage is, of course, the increase in litigation concerning classification societies' liabilities.

The second possible solution for changing the present situation involves stricter rules combined with some sort of cooperation between the classification societies, thus preventing the owners 'shopping around', not because the service is better and not because one classification society is cheaper than the other, but only because it is easier for the owner to get his vessel approved by one classification society than the other.

ANDERS ULRIK

CHAPTER 4

UK AND FAR EAST PERSPECTIVE

Figures published by the Salvage Association report that between 1978 and 1990 43 log carriers were lost and 20 were wrecked. Figures published by Lloyd's Register in May 1991 show that 34 bulkers were either lost or seriously structurally damaged since 1990. In the five months since May 1991 a further eight bulkers have been lost. Losses of bulk carriers to October 1991 exceeded those in the whole of 1990. These casualties led to the loss of 125 lives in 1990 and 148 lives in 1991.

In response to these sobering statistics, a debate has arisen as to whether these losses are the consequence of age, cargo handling procedures, corrosion, design fault, human error or a combination of all five. The classification societies have been invited to make proposals as to how shipping losses may be reduced and their initiatives have been welcomed by the industry. The result is that there is now a call upon classification societies to perform a more extensive role than that portrayed by their traditional functions such as hull and machinery surveys and the issue of class certificates.

For example, three major classification societies have cooperated with five leading ship management companies to produce a quality assurance system for ship management. Some societies launched a 'safety management class' in 1989, designed to monitor safety and pollution control. Owners are invited to enter into this class on a voluntary basis. The class operates as a supplement to the vessel's Hull and Machinery Class Notation and provides the ship owner with a documented technical evaluation of his fleet. This class will also assess management systems both on board and in owners' and managers' offices ashore. LR also operates a voluntary 'condition assessment hull scheme', involving renovation to first or second survey status and a ship management certification scheme.

More recently, the IACS has resolved to form a working party to exchange data on casualties and set up a quality system certification programme. This envisages the introduction of a quality control system for Members of the IACS which conforms with standards (ISO9001) which have been agreed by all societies. These standards will be enforced by initial and periodic audits so as to monitor the performance of member classification societies. Compliance with the new code will be compulsory in order to maintain membership of the IACS.

Classification societies are therefore extending their role beyond the technical to the operational and managerial aspects of the shipping business. This, no doubt, is a reflection of the fact that human error is now believed to account for a significant proportion of shipping casualties.

In the offshore field, classification societies play a leading role as the certifying authority for the government departments with responsibility for licensing offshore platforms' operations. For example, in the UK, LR are the certifying authority for the Department of Energy. At the same time LR has also become involved in advising and reviewing platform owners' and operators' safety assessments.

One of the few statements upon which politicians (and royalty) are likely to agree is that the higher the profile the greater the degree of accountability. Whether this is due to public demand, pressure from shipowners, hull underwriters or P&I Clubs, outbursts from politicians or environmentalists or in response to a directive from the societies' financial directors, classification societies are taking on increasingly greater roles in advisory and supervisory capacities in the shipping industry. The development of this role necessarily leads to an enquiry as to how the performance of the classification societies themselves is to be monitored.

As with any association of manufacturers, society of professional men or guild of craftsmen, the IACS and its members will wish to ensure that the standards of their profession are maintained. The public at large, the shipping industry and its customers will also need to be satisfied that the machinery exists to keep those controls in check.

This need is far removed from any desire to transfer liability for the safe operation of the shipping and offshore industries to classification societies or to convert classification societies into the industry's insurers. In the field of classification, the attending classification surveyor is necessarily given a wide area of discretion when conducting his survey. Nevertheless human error may occur in this field, as in any other.

The modern view is likely to lead to the question as to whether there is any reason why the classification societies should enjoy a greater degree of immunity or unaccountability than any other profession engaged in or on the fringe of the shipping community.

Professional standards can be monitored in a number of different ways.

Self policing

The IACS has been formed and has announced the introduction of its own standards. However not all classification societies are members of the IACS. Self policing would, however, be one possibility if membership was sufficiently widespread to extend to all national classification societies. Examples of self policing are found in a number of institutions, such as the Synod of the Church of England.

Regulation by means of accountability through the civil courts

Examples are plumbers, electricians, and estate agents none of whom need to belong to a professional body under UK or Hong Kong law.

A hybrid system

Examples in other professions are the British Medical Association or the Law Society which maintain the professional standards of the UK's doctors and solicitors and which impose disciplinary measures when necessary. Such disciplinary procedures are independent of any civil liability.

A grant of immunity from civil action

This could be made either on the grounds that the profession performs a quasi-executive role of government, or on the grounds that the professional body is a charitable institution and should therefore in some way be set above the law rather like, to date, commercial arbitrators.

So far as the UK courts are concerned, whose decisions are likely to be followed in Hong Kong, Singapore, Malaysia and Brunei, the tendency to date has been to adopt the fourth option and to cloak the classification societies with immunity. Why has this occurred? The answer appears to have been partly one of policy and partly a question of law.

There have in fact been very few cases involving claims against classification societies reported by the UK courts. In theory such claims could be brought either in contract or in tort. So far as contract is concerned, it is fair to say that there are no reported decisions on such a claim at all. This is most likely due to the very stringent conditions which are imposed by classification societies on their customers, the shipowners, with whom they enter into a contract to provide classification status. For example, survey reports issued by NKK state:

> This report is issued subject to the condition that it is understood and agreed that neither the society nor any of its Committees is under any circumstances whatever to be held responsible for any inaccuracy in any report or certificate issued by the Society or its Surveyors or in any entry in the Record or other publication of the Society or for any error of judgment, default or negligence of its Officers, Surveyors or Agents.

It is self-evident that this wording is extremely wide. In almost all cases when faced with this type of wording the owners will assume, probably correctly, that they have no claim against the classification society.

If put to the test however various questions would arise. For example:

— Have the terms of the exclusion clause been agreed by owners? If they were agreed were they agreed before the survey was carried out? Were they agreed before the survey report was commissioned or received or a verbal report given?

— In extreme cases, has there been a total absence or failure of consideration on the part of the classification society?
— Does the precise wording protect the society in all eventualities? For example, depending on the facts of the case does the wording exclude liability for omissions?
— Does the clause rule out a claim in tort? (See *Midland Banker Trust Company.*[1])
— Would the clause protect the classification society when acting in its capacity as state certifying authority, if faced with a claim by the appointing state? What would be the attitude for example of a vessel's flag state whose coastline was polluted as a result of a causative error or omission on the part of the classification surveyor assigned by that state to enforce their own safety certification requirements?

The position in tort is less clear. A claim in tort would normally be brought where there is no contract between the claimant and the classification society. This could arise, for example, in the event of a claim by: a vessel's crew and their dependents following a casualty involving loss of life; the vessel's charterers; the vessel's managers; owners of property damaged by the vessel such as a colliding vessel or by owners of other property; and, to draw from the example mentioned previously, the owners of a polluted coastline. Similarly a vessel's buyers could only sue the seller's classification society, if at all, in tort.

One of the most recent examples of an attempt to recover from a classification society arose in the case of the *Morning Watch.*[2] The *Morning Watch* was a steel hull motor yacht built in 1962 according to Lloyd's Register of Shipping Rules issued in 1958. She was regularly surveyed in accordance with class rules which required biennial surveys and a special survey every four years. In October 1984, some time prior to the next special survey due date, LR were requested by the owners to carry out a special survey as the vessel was to be sold early next season. The vessel was inspected by a LR surveyor (who had inspected the vessel on a previous survey) and in November 1984 he issued an interim certificate that the vessel be credited with passing special survey when listed repairs had been effected. These repairs consisted largely of rectifying localised areas of corrosion.

In March 1985 LR approved the surveyor's recommendations, the interim certificate was issued and sent to the owners' agent who then advertised the sale of the yacht mentioning 'always maintained to 100 A1 at Lloyd's . . . has passed current special survey (November 1984) with no difficulty so purchaser is spared expense of a survey'.

A buyer then enquired as to the vessel's precise survey position and made an offer for the vessel on 'as is where is' terms in February 1985 (i.e. before Lloyd's had approved the attending surveyor's recommendation) and without requesting or having sight of the temporary or the interim certificate. Since, however, the

1. *Midland Banker Trust Co* v. *Hett Stubbs & Kemp* [1979] Ch 384.
2. *Mariola Marine Corporation* v. *Lloyd's Register of Shipping* [1990] 1 Lloyd's Rep. 547.

vessel was to be refitted by the buyer the surveyor issued an interim certificate recommending deferment of the remaining repairs pending modifications by the buyers. The proposed modifications included fitting a substantial breakwater forward of the deck house. When those modifications began and the deck planking was removed an additional and previously undetected area of corrosion was disclosed. The buyers then sued LR arguing that the yacht had serious defects rendering her unseaworthy and that these defects should have been detected by the attending surveyor. The plaintiff's claim therefore was for damages for economic loss suffered as a result of relying on alleged misstatements negligently made by LR. The court held that LR was not liable to the purchasers. Even so the judge arrived at the following conclusions:

- Where the classification society issues a class certificate, that act may well carry with it representations as to the condition of the classified vessel.
- Where a third party makes some representation as to the class of the vessel, that representation amounts to no more than the statement of the classification status of the vessel.
- As there was no contract between the buyers and LR, liability could only arise if there was a breach of a duty of care owed by the classification society to the purchaser.

For a duty of care to exist the following conditions had to exist: it must be reasonably foreseeable to the classification society that the plaintiff was liable to rely on his statement; there must be the necessary 'proximity' between the classification society and the plaintiff; and it must be 'just and reasonable' in all the circumstances to impose a duty of care.

The judge held that the buyers had satisfied the first requirement. Although LR did not have the actual purchaser in contemplation, they had been informed that the vessel was to be sold and it was reasonably foreseeable that the purchaser would be influenced by the results of the survey work.

The purchaser failed on the second leg, however, in that he did not establish a sufficient degree of proximity between the classification society and the purchaser. This is a difficult concept to grasp and, in the words of the judge, 'the requirement can be described but not defined'. In practice, however, the judge seems to have concluded that the degree of proximity was not present largely on the grounds of policy. In his own words: 'to accept the general proposition that LR owes a duty of care to those foreseeably liable to suffer economic loss in consequence of reliance on the negligent classification of a vessel would be to make a substantial further advance in the law of negligence.'

As a result it was unnecessary for the court to go any further because there was insufficient proximity between the purchaser and the classification society and the court did not have to consider whether the exclusion in LR's conditions was wide enough to protect the classification society for such a claim.

Does this case therefore sound the death knell for claims against classification societies? Possibly not. Any one of the following factors, if different, could cause a judge to decide the question of liability differently:

— *The Morning Watch* was a case concerned with economic loss only. The general tendency of the UK courts is to restrict liability in tort for economic loss. The position of a claimant who has suffered physical loss or damage as a result of professional negligence is far stronger. (See *D & F Estates Ltd*[3] and *Muirhead.*[4])
— The purchaser bought the *Morning Watch* on 'as is where is' terms. He at no stage inspected the vessel or the classification certificates prior to entering into the contract to purchase the yacht.
— The purchaser was not paying either directly or indirectly, the fees of the classification society (Cf *Smith* v. *Bush Note*[5].)
— The classification society was not aware of the buyer's identity and made no statement directly to the buyer. The position would be more difficult to assess where there is direct correspondence or communication between the potential purchaser and the classification society prior to the sale being concluded.
— Some, but not all, classification societies have a charitable status. In the case of LR the judge took note of the society's charitable status and found their principal purpose was to 'enhance the safety of life and property at sea', rather than to protect the economic interests of those involved, in one role or another, within the shipping industry. Not all classification societies may be run as charities however. Moreover, classification societies are spreading their wings to encompass certification of management systems. Will it be accurate to say that future classification society activities are not concerned with economic livelihood or the commercial success of their customers?
— The survey of the *Morning Watch*, which it is alleged was negligently carried out, was not done for the purpose of selling the yacht. The survey was simply an incident in the regular schedule of inspections involved in keeping the *Morning Watch* in class with LR. The position might be different if the seller and the purchaser together instructed the classification society to survey the vessel with the sale in mind.

The Morning Watch is not going to appeal. The judge concluded that the yacht contained defects which should have been detected by the classification surveyor and that the class surveyor was negligent in failing to detect corrosion by way of the engine room entering the galley and the exhaust truck compartment. He also held that the purchasers were not guilty of contributory negligence for relying on the special survey and not carrying out their own survey instead purchasing the vessel on 'as is' terms. The facts of the next case for consideration by the court

3. *D & F Estates Ltd* v. *Church Commissioners for England* [1989] AC 177.
4. *Muirhead* v. *Industrial Tank Specialities Ltd* [1986] QB 507 (CA).
5. *Smith* v. *Bush* [1989] 2 WLR 790 (HL).

could be very different and recent case law suggests that those providing professional services can be made liable for economic loss. The House of Lords has decided in *Smith* v. *Bush*[5] that a real estate surveyor engaged by a bank to value property for the purposes of a loan to a purchaser, whose fees are paid by the purchaser, will be liable in tort to the purchaser for any negligent valuation given to the bank. That situation is not so very far removed from that of the purchaser of the *Morning Watch*. Moreover two recent House of Lords decisions, *Murphy*[6] and *Bates*[7], which reduce the scope of tortious liability under UK law, have no immediate impact upon the potential liability of surveyors particularly where there is physical damage.

In *Murphy*, the House of Lords ruled that a local housing authority was not liable to purchasers of a building for economic loss suffered as a result of negligent advice given to the local authority by a civil engineer. In *Bates*, lessees of a building were unable to recover from structural surveyors the cost of repairs and the dislocation to premises which required repairs as a result of incorrect construction. From these cases, however, it seems that the principles laid down in *Hedley Byrne*[8] are likely to assume increasing importance since those (potential liability of a professional adviser) survive the House of Lords decisions in *Murphy* and *Bates*. The result is that a distinction is drawn between acts and statements. Thus the builder of a vessel or an office block may have no liability in negligence to third parties for doing working inadequately but if he inaccurately certifies the construction as being adequate or complying with certain prescribed requirements he will be liable under the *Hedley Byrne* principle.

A greater role for classification societies in preventive measures is to be welcomed. The introduction of internal quality control procedures by the IACS is also welcomed as would be a directive by state certifying authorities to their national classification societies requiring compulsory membership of the IACS. Self regulation is the ideal form of control, but to err is human and classification societies, as with any other professionals, should not shy away from responding to criticism if made and, if necessary, meeting their liability in the civil courts. *The Morning Watch* does not tell the whole story.

CHRIS MOORE

6. *Murphy* v. *Brentwood District Council* [1990] 3 WLR 414.
7. *Department of the Environment* v. *Bates* [1990] 3 WLR 457.
8. *Hedley Byrne* v. *Heller* [1964] AC 465.

CHAPTER 5

US PERSPECTIVE

In that today's classification societies render a wide variety of services which touch nearly every facet of maritime activity, the impact they have on the safety of the world's vessels is enormous. With the increase in statutory certification services, as distinct from the more traditional classification services with which the societies have always been identified, the ensuing change in circumstances opens the door to new possibilities for liability.

The International Convention for the Safety of Life at Sea (SOLAS) and the International Convention on Load Lines (Load-Lines) were drafted by representatives from well over 50 countries in order to protect life and property from risk of serious harm. A perusal of the two conventions reveals dozens upon dozens of sophisticated technical requirements governing the design, construction and operation of ocean-going vessels. These requirements concern life-saving appliances, structural integrity, radio communications, damage stability and many other aspects of maritime transportation, all of which deserve serious attention.

The recent incident off the South African coast involving the cruise ship *Oceanos* highlights the importance of ship safety. Hundreds needed rescuing by helicopter and some passengers chose to jump into open waters with nothing but their life jackets and ended up drifting for miles. Surprisingly, all survived this disaster.

The SOLAS and Load-Lines Conventions were intended to prevent disasters like the *Oceanos*. A ship in compliance with their technical requirements is endowed with safety characteristics which tend to make casualties far less likely and minimise the loss of life and property when they do occur. If every ship in the world were in compliance with SOLAS and Load-Lines, there would be very few tragedies involving sinking vessels.

But, unfortunately, many of the world's vessels, including cruise ships, are not in compliance with SOLAS and Load-Lines, even though the conventions' provisions have been incorporated into the national laws of almost all the countries which sent representatives to draft them. How could there be so many violations of these conventions? How can the public, as it boards cruise ships like the *Oceanos*, have confidence that its ships are safe? How can the law help to reduce the number of vessels—especially cruise ships—which are not in compliance? The answers to these questions have roots in the almost exclusive method by which the world community has decided to enforce conventions.

There are two very important features to both international agreements that have a lot to do with the generation of an unacceptably high number of ships failing to meet the conventions' requirements. These ostensibly innocuous provisions have created an atmosphere in which we see a high incidence of 'fitting the rules to the vessel instead of fitting the vessel to the rules' (as was reported in a relatively recent National Transportation Safety Board report).

In the first place, both conventions carry broad expressions of reciprocity as they lay out the terms of enforcement. It is important to remember that conventions like SOLAS and Load-Lines do not have the weight of law *per se*. They are non-self-executing treaties: they enjoy actual legal effect only by being included among the national laws of those countries which assembled to draft them. A convention may be thought to resemble a contract formed by the countries which are signatories to it. A signatory country agrees to take all of the convention's terms and make them part of its own national law in exchange for promises from all the other signatory nations that they will do likewise. For instance, the USA is a signatory to both the SOLAS and Load-Lines Conventions, and a careful reading of the US Code and the Code of Federal Regulations will uncover all the technical and not-so-technical requirements of both conventions. These requirements have been incorporated into US law as the conventions dictate. They apply to nearly all ships making use of US ports and nearly all ships flying the US flag.

But how does the US treat a vessel flying the flag of a fellow signatory when that vessel visits a US port? The fellow signatory has already examined the vessel to enforce the requirements of the conventions. Should the US conduct another examination to determine compliance? After all, the convention-inspired US laws apply to all vessels making use of US ports. To what extent can the US Coast Guard, as an enforcement agency, pass judgment upon another signatory's enforcement of the conventions?

These questions return to the earlier reference to 'broad expressions of reciprocity'. Under both conventions, the USA (and any other host signatory for that matter) must accept another signatory's valid certificate of compliance as sufficient evidence of compliance when the foreign signatory's vessel visits a US port. For example, when a cruise ship flying the Bahamian flag visits Miami to embark hundreds of US tourists, the US Coast Guard, basically, must accept the Bahamian certificates as sufficient evidence of compliance and not conduct any comprehensive surveys of its own. The Coast Guard is bound to accept the Bahamian determination that the vessel complies with the terms of the conventions. This is so even though the Bahamian cruise ship must, technically, comply with those terms as a matter of US law when it visits a US port.

Combined with this broad expression of reciprocity is a second feature common to both conventions which makes it more likely that ships are not in compliance with the requirements. This second feature permits signatory nations to authorise private entities to perform the inspections and issue the certificates necessitated by the conventions. These private entities are almost always classification societies.

The societies clamour for authorisations from the many signatory nations for a very important reason: they charge shipowners substantial fees for conducting inspections and issuing certificates under the conventions. The signatories are eager to authorise societies to perform these services because these countries are often uninterested in providing the financial support for an equivalent to the US Coast Guard. In fact, the USA, with all of its budget woes, has even participated in the rush to authorise societies to perform these enforcement services. Today, ABS performs nearly all of the Load-Lines inspections and certifications on behalf of the USA for US flag vessels.

But what if a country authorises more than one classification society to perform statutory (Load-Lines and SOLAS) certifications? Society A wants shipowner X's business just as much as Society B. Which society will X choose to perform these services? Will X choose the society which charges less for the services (and maybe spends less on them too)? Will X choose the society which is more eager to please a shipowner (by perhaps showing more lenience when it comes to the enforcement of the conventions—a lenience that means fewer expensive changes must be made to a vessel before it is certified and therefore able to make use of the world's ports)? If X chooses Society A to perform these services the first time and X feels that A may have charged too much or have been too stringent in the enforcement of the conventions, which society do you think X will choose next time?

It should not be forgotten that a lot of money is at stake when a shipowner hires a society to perform certification services. Classification societies have been reporting revenues of hundreds of millions of dollars. For example, ABS, a 'non-profit corporation', reported a net income of more than $11m on operating revenues of $122m just last year. Charging fees for the enforcement of international conventions—compliance with which is required as a matter of law by most of the nations in global maritime commerce—has become big business for classification societies.

So what there is today (with regard to the enforcement of international conventions drafted specifically to protect life and property from risk of serious harm) is a system in which classification societies, money-making entities, vie with one another for fees from shipowners for the performance of certification services which entail the enforcement of national laws designed to protect life and property. In short, the world community has countenanced the merging of governmental obligations to protect the public from undue risks of harm with market incentives which can blind many to the need for enhancement of the general welfare. This marriage of the governmental angel with the capitalistic devil can threaten proper enforcement of the conventions. There is no more poignant set of circumstances than the one which pertains to the enforcement of conventions aboard cruise ships.

Every year hundreds of thousands of tourists board cruise ships. These tourists have no means by which they can ascertain whether a ship is as safe as they might want it to be. Many times, a vast percentage of a cruise ship's passengers have never been aboard a ship, never seen the ocean. How are these people supposed to assure themselves that their ship has the proper levels of structural integrity, damage stability, life-saving capacity, and radio communications? How do these people know this is not another *Oceanos*?

The answer, of course, should be that these people can look to the SOLAS and Load-Line Conventions for reassurance. This would mean that the passengers must rely upon money-making entities to enforce international safety requirements intended to protect people just like them. The passengers must rely upon classification societies that may be distracted by the lure of money and by the related desire to please their customers, the shipowners.

In a nightmarish sequence which has never and probably will never occur, it is possible to imagine Shipowner X sitting down to negotiate the terms of its certification services contract with Society B. Having had an unpleasant experience with Society A (X thought the fees were too high and the enforcement too stringent and expensive), Shipowner X explains to Society B that X wishes to pay lower fees and cannot understand the blinkered mentality of at least one classification society's surveyors. Without asking for an explicit compromise of the quality of the services, X simply communicates its natural desire to pay as little for these necessities as possible. Feeling the pressure not only of a declining maritime industry but also of intense competition within the ranks of societies, Society B presents Shipowner X with a contract having the following two ingredients: the fees are lower than those charged by Society A; and there is a hold-harmless clause which says that Society B will, basically, not be held liable for its own negligence. Shipowner X, seeing the lower fees, grabs this opportunity and before long the inspections have been conducted, certificates issued, and fees paid. The ship has been certified under both the Load-Lines and SOLAS Conventions.

All signatories are obliged to accept the classification society's authorised certificate as sufficient evidence of compliance whenever the ship visits signatories' ports. And no one is ever quite sure if the profit motive, especially in the absence of any liability for negligent performance, has affected the way in which the society deemed the ship to be in actual compliance with both conventions.

The hold-harmless clause referred to in the hypothetical case is now common among the contracts offered by classification societies. The societies seem bent on protecting themselves from all liabilities in the event that they fail to perform their services in a non-negligent manner.

Courts have seemed more and more willing to honour hold-harmless clauses in recent years. In the USA, at least, courts have strongly endorsed the proposition that sophisticated commercial entities should negotiate over allocation of risk of loss via their contracts and be held accountable for those allocations. Not only does such a system encourage efficiency according to popular economic models, but it also reduces the caseloads of sometimes overburdened courts. Essential to this endorsement of contractual allocation of risk of loss is that commerical entities be prohibited from suing each other in tort for negligent performance (or breach) of a contract. This is amply expressed by the US Supreme Court's 1986 *East River* decision[1].

But if the classification societies are never to be held liable for their own negligence in the inspection, enforcement, and certification of vessels under international conventions, how do the passengers know that the conventions' terms are properly enforced? Who protects the passengers' interests?

First, it is declared, the shipowner has a non-delegable duty to maintain the seaworthiness of his vessel. He should be the one with the responsibility of making sure his vessel complies with the requirements of the conventions as he should have the greatest incentive to see to it that his ship displays the safety characteristics that protect him from liability and protect his property interests.

Two responses can be made to the assertion that the shipowner's non-delegable duty to maintain seaworthiness is a sufficient protection of passengers' interests *vis-à-vis* implementation of the conventions' terms. (Both are in addition to the simple response that shipowners are usually quite heavily insured.)

First, the terms of SOLAS and Load-Lines are quite sophisticated and require close study over a long period of time before they can be properly applied. Shipowners would have to know advanced naval architecture and marine engineering if the non-delegable duty rule required them to board vessels to verify compliance with international conventions. This is why shipowners pay classification societies large fees. Societies are sufficiently familiar with the engineering concepts to make sense of the requirements and they possess the erudition and experience necessary for meaningful application of SOLAS and Load-Lines. The non-delegable duty rule directs itself more towards ensuring that injured parties will have deep pockets from which to retrieve adequate recoveries. For this reason shipowners may not use the hiring of a society as a defence to the charge that the vessel was unseaworthy. But after the shipowner has paid injured parties and suffered his own loss, why bar him from suing commercial entities whose negligence caused his damages?

The second reason as to why the shipowner is an inadequate protector of the public's interest in making sure conventions are properly enforced is that the shipowner will always be tempted to perceive compliance in the way that minimises his costs. In some instances spending money on safety requirements may be the most cost effective measure, if it avoids catastrophic loss in the future. Unfortunately, the cost of many safety requirements cannot be justified economically. Yet, well over 50 nations assembled to draft the conventions for the very reason that economics should not determine the extent to which a vessel carries safety features. The public requires more protection than that which

1. *East River SS Corp* v. *Transamerica Delaval Inc*, 476 US 858, 106 S. Ct 2295, L. Ed. 2nd 855 (1986).

emerges from unbridled interaction of economic forces. An entity other than the shipowner must make sure the conventions' requirements are met. Shipowners cannot be expected to have the technical resources nor the economic motivation to do so.

The other major party which can look out for the public welfare is the authorising flag state. It can monitor the extent to which its chosen classification societies are performing competently. Then, it can take appropriate action after determining that a society has abused its authorisation. Director-General Torkild R. Funder recently said the following in this regard:

> From experiences of port state control over recent years, and investigations of some of the accidents that have taken place, it seems that some flag states may have failed in doing what is expected of them in regard to control of their ships.
>
> It is argued by some countries that such incidents are in no way their fault. It is either the master and his crew who have failed to fulfil their responsibilities or it is the classification society, entrusted by the flag state to carry out a survey, which has failed. This may be so in some cases, but in other cases it may be argued that the flag state, which still has ultimate responsibility, has failed in exercising control or of auditing what was done by the other parties.

Holding flag states to a higher duty of care is an unrealistic way of protecting the public interest in that it is unrealistic to expect many of the flag states to develop the expertise and bureaucracy necessary to monitor the performance of classification societies. Again, societies are in possession of rather arcane and demanding naval architectural principles. These are not notions which can be absorbed overnight. Further, training a regiment of persons to monitor inspections conducted by societies worldwide is a task beyond the financial means of many flags of convenience and only the large, wealthy nations could effectively inspect and certify vessels. Many of the vessels which serve the third world would necessarily lose whatever levels of safety they are forced to manifest today.

Perhaps the shipowner and the flag state are inadequate protectors of the public trust. If societies were exposed to significant civil liability for negligent performance of their services, there would probably be far fewer unsafe vessels. The societies would be motivated by a sufficient incentive to ensure that they did their jobs properly—and that they did not yield to the economic temptations to neglect their duties.

In the USA there are already a good number of players in society who are not permitted to shield themselves from liability for negligence in the rendering of their services. This prohibition against use of disclaimers of liability or hold-harmless clauses is usually applied to professions which implicate the public trust to a high degree. For instance, it is unethical in the USA for a lawyer to render legal services to a client under a contract which holds the lawyer harmless for his negligence. If a corporation retained an attorney to inspect its plant for violations of work safety regulations, and the attorney was negligent in the performance of these services, the corporation—even though it, of course, is primarily responsible for compliance with such regulations—could conceivably sue the attorney for malpractice in the event of the corporation suffering damages due to non-compliance. This kind of delegation of work should become more and more common as man dreams up more and more sophisticated ways to regulate his business.

It is important to remember that societies exposed to liability would not become insurers of the vessels they inspected and certified. First, like attorneys, they would only be held liable for their negligence—not for every mistake they made. Secondly, it would be incumbent upon the disappointed shipowner to show that a society's negligence was the proximate cause of the damage. This would become especially difficult as time passed between the inspection and the occurrence which served as the focus of the complaint. But where a shipowner could show he suffered harm due to the negligence of a classification society, the classification society would always be held liable (like an attorney). Thus the public would be assured that international conventions designed to protect people like them from risk of serious harm would be enforced by entities always motivated by an appropriate fear of significant liability.

Such constant exposure to civil liability ought to exist for statutory certifications of all vessels, cruise ships as well as those primarily devoted to cargo. In the event that the industry cannot accommodate such broad classification society liability, it may be possible to limit the application of this kind of professional civil liability to those situations in which a classification society performs statutory certifications for passenger ships. The public deserves as much, and the world need not witness another *Oceanos*.

BRIAN D. STARER

CHAPTER 6

GERMAN PERSPECTIVE: IN DEFENCE OF CLASSIFICATION SOCIETIES

INTRODUCTION

A multitude of recent court cases against classification societies raises the question as to whether a third party, who is not the contractual partner, may bring a claim for damages against a classification society on the basis of the representations made in a class certificate. In the majority of cases suit is brought not by the shipowner as the party contracting with the classification society, but by a third party standing outside the contractual relationship between the shipowner and the classification society. In theory, these might be cargo interests, charterers, mortgagees or underwriters. However, in practice, leaving aside the *Yarrawonga* case, in which the hull underwriters appear as plaintiffs, nearly all other cases concern a buyer of the subject ship. Therefore by focusing on the role of classification societies in connection with the sale of vessels it is important to discern whether or not the classification society is liable to the buyer of a vessel in the case of issuance of incorrect certificates, even though at the material time the buyer does not have a contract with the classification society.

In the past this problem never arose. Like a pilot, a classification society would never be sued—this was just not done. Times have changed however. We now see a number of liability actions against classification societies, some of which are presently pending in German courts.

THE ROLE OF CLASSIFICATION SOCIETIES

The purpose and functions of a classification society are unfortunately frequently misunderstood, and such misunderstandings lead to unmeritorious and therefore unnecessary litigation. In short:

- A classification society, acting as a supervisory body, will examine the safety of a ship in accordance with certain very well defined and exactly formulated classification rules. This supervisory function is performed exclusively in the interests of safety for ship and crew. Economic interests are of no importance.
- The following types of surveys have to be distinguished:

periodic surveys
damage-and-repair surveys
surveys in dry docks
particular surveys with a specially defined scope.

- Only in the case of periodic surveys (annual and special surveys) will there be a generic examination of the ship according to certain check lists.
- Certificates such as 'class confirmed' relate, in the case of particular surveys with a specially defined scope, to that special scope and, in the case of periodic surveys, only to those parts which, according to the classification rules, have to be examined.
- The shipowners are contractually obliged to notify the classification society of any defects which might impair the class.
- There are many areas in a ship which have nothing whatsoever to do with class.

To know and to observe these fundamental principles is of paramount importance when considering the question of liability. These principles provide the framework within which the liability of a classification society, if any, may be discussed.

In 1907 the German Imperial Court and in 1972 the District Court in Hamburg dismissed an action brought by a shipowner against his contracting partner, the classification society. Of course, these decisions were partly based on legal reasoning which is considered today to be no longer applicable. However, they were also based on the ideal—which is still applicable today—that the classification society examines a ship with regard to safety and seaworthiness, but in applying its rules, it must not be mistaken as guaranteeing for its contractual partner, the shipowner, that a third party (in both cases a shipyard) has fully complied with his contractual obligations. Following a similar line of reasoning, the Federal Supreme Court in 1973 ruled that the TÜV (the Technischer Überwachungsverein), an institution similar to the classification society but which deals with periodic technical surveys of motor cars, is concerned solely with maintaining the safety of road traffic in the interest of the general public. In particular, it is not the task of the TÜV to ensure that the purchaser of a motor car does not suffer financial loss as a result of buying a defective vehicle.

This really is the heart of the matter. Just like the TÜV, the classification society is exclusively concerned with safety aspects in shipping. It is not the job of the society to ensure that its contracting partner, the shipowner—and even less any third part—suffers purely financial loss.

In addition, one has to bear in mind that many classification societies, for instance the Germanischer Lloyd (GL), are by their corporate structure designed to serve the general public. According to the Articles of Association of GL only an aggregate of DM 12,000 out of the profit of the company can be distributed amongst the shareholders. Any profit beyond this comparatively small sum, accruing to a company with a work force of roughly 1,000 employees, is devoted to scientific and technical research which forms one of the prime objectives of the company. Save for this fraction mentioned, the entire profit of the company is re-invested in ship-related science and technology. Moreover, the activities of any classification society are, on the one hand, prone to substantial risks, on the other they are remunerated by relatively modest fees. Liability insurance cover is hardly affordable in view of the massive potential liabilities. In view of this it may be claimed with justification that, under German law, a classification society should be entitled to limit its liability in its general terms and conditions. Under German law the contract concluded between a classification society and a shipowner would be qualified as a contract for services rendered. If these services are defective then the contractual partner has a claim against the classification society either for rescission of the contract or for reduction of the agreed remuneration. If in addition the classification society is guilty of negligence in causing such defects, then the shipowner as the contracting partner is entitled to damages. However, under German law this claim to damages can be excluded by contract so long as the rights to rescind the contract or to demand a reduction in the agreed remuneration are maintained.

LIABILITY VIS-À-VIS THIRD PARTIES

As shown, any liability of the classification society *vis-à-vis* the shipowner under the contract may be reduced or even excluded by contract. This being so, there should be all the more reason to permit such exclusion of liability *vis-à-vis* a third, non-contracting party such as, for instance, the purchaser of the ship.

When faced with this issue in 1907, the Imperial Court did away with this problem in a relatively simple manner: it rejected contractual claims immediately and looked more closely at claims in tort.

The latter were also rejected because the plaintiff could not establish that the classification society had acted with intent to cause harm. There were no other legal grounds on which a claim for damages sustained by the third party, could have been based. There was no contractual relationship betwee the classification society and the third party. Today it is sometimes argued that there 'springs to life' a contract for the supply of information between the classification society and the buyer. However, this rather contrived legal construction collapses if one looks at the fact that, in general, classification societies, according to their rules, are neither authorised nor willing to give to third parties information about the ship.

Unlike most common law jurisdictions there exists under German law the concept of a contract for the benefit of third parties. One category within that concept is a contract with 'protective effect' in favour of third parties. This category was initially conceived by German courts in cases involving contractual duties of care, particularly in the context of family law. According to these principles, a third party which has not entered into a contractual relationship with the debtor might nevertheless be permitted contractual claims against the debtor, alongside the creditor himself. However, this 'protective umbrella' in favour of the third party presupposes that, according to the intention of the debtor and the creditor as the contracting parties, the contract is also to generate a protective effect with regard to the third party. Initially, this prerequisite was thought to exist only if it was somehow incumbent on the creditor to look after the personal protection of the third party. For instance, a tenant naturally has to look after the interests of the members of his family living with him in his house, which means that the landlord owes a duty of care arising from the contract of lease to those family members in the same way as towards the tenant himself. More recently, this legal reasoning has been extended to cover chartered accountants, tax advisers and consultants who issue certificates, for instance with regard to the commercial value of an enterprise or of real property, such certificates being designed to form the basis for somebody's decision to purchase the company or the real estate. Before prospective buyers can impliedly be covered by such a contract it has to be established that:

- the third party 'stands close' to the main contractual obligation;
- the creditor also has a strong interest in protecting this third party;
- both the above conditions must have been known to the debtor;
- the position of the third party must be such as to deserve special protection.

Subject to the above conditions, it is arguable that third parties do enjoy the 'protective umbrella' of a contract between two other parties in exceptional circumstances.

First, in applying these principles to the sale of a vessel one immediately notes that the interest of the seller, being himself the contractual partner of the classification society, is completely different from that of the buyer. As the seller has to pay for repairs he is not at all interested in having such defects detected by the classification society. However, it is the seller and not the buyer who calls in and pays the classification society. By contrast, the buyer is of course very keen that the classification society should detect many faults because, as long as he has not taken delivery of the ship, he can demand that the seller rectify them.

Already this evident clash of interests between seller and buyer provides a strong argument against extending to the buyer the 'protective umbrella' of a contract concluded between the seller and the classification society.

Secondly, in all cases as yet decided or still pending in Germany the buyers have purchased relatively old ships at prices duly adjusted to the age and condition of the vessel. Yet, when making a claim against the classification society, based on an allegedly wrong certificate, the claim figure came to between 50 per cent and more than 100 per cent of the purchase price. Therefore, there are serious misgivings about extending the concept of the third party contract.

Thirdly, when thc courts came to consider the liability of chartered accountants, tax advisers and the other consultants with regard to buying and selling companies or real property, those cases usually involved buyers who did not have available to them the requisite information and expertise to form their own judgment with regard to the value of the subject company or property. The buyers therefore had no choice but to rely on the advice and reports of the sellers' consultants. The position with regard to the sale of a ship is different:

- The purchaser, most often a shipowner himself, has a very good look at the ship before he buys. He brings in his own experts. He is given an opportunity to examine the ship down to her last details.
- The purchaser requests that the classification files be examined by experts. He knows everything about the history of the ship (average damage, groundings, collisions etc).
- The purchaser uses those defects in order to negotiate a lower price.
- Only afterwards does the purchaser enter into a contract, usually on the basis of the Norwegian Saleform 'as she is at the time of inspection'.
- Instead of insisting at least on a class renewal the purchaser is usually content with a class confirmed certificate and in many cases he is not even aware that in some cases certificates of this kind are issued after inspecting the classification files, rather than inspecting the ship herself!
- In clause 11 of the Norwegian Sale form the purchaser assumes the risk that the seller has not complied with his obligation to inform the classification society with regard to any defects which might affect the vessel's class as, naturally, the seller feels little incentive to comply with this obligation.

The above items clearly outline the distinction between the case of buying a company or piece of property on the basis of a balance sheet or a tax consultant's report and the case of buying a ship. Unlike the former case, the buyer of a ship does not merit protection. He does not rely on the certificate of the classification society; he knows the ship himself, her history and her present condition, in many cases better than the classification society. He uses that knowledge when negotiating a cheaper price. He then waives all warranties with regard to fitness and seaworthiness. Then, later on, he draws on the classification society for the pursuit of his commercial objectives by calling upon it to put right defects which he had knowingly accepted *vis-à-vis* the seller in the first place. For this purpose the buyer not infrequently tries to establish contact with the classification society a few days before the date scheduled for delivery, informs the society about all the defects he has discovered with the aid of his experts, and thereby tries to persuade the classification society to force the seller to put right these defects.

Fourthly, it is a peculiar fact that in many cases the plaintiff's submissions state that he knew each and every defect of the vessel prior to taking delivery and tried to persuade the classification society to have them rectified. It is clear that the purchaser in such a case did not rely on the class certificate.

Fifthly, under German law the buyer, as the plaintiff, has to contend that under the MOA on the basis of the Norwegian Sale form—which is normally subject to English law—he was obliged to take delivery of the ship even though he knew perfectly well about her defects, simply because the seller submitted a 'clean' class certificate. Under German law it is clearly not the condition of the certificate, but the condition of the vessel that matters. If the ship is not up to the contractually warranted condition, the buyer may refuse to take delivery irrespective of whether or not the ship is tendered with clean certificates.

Finally, assuming for the moment that even under English law the buyer is not obliged to take delivery of a defective ship with clean certificates, then he does not suffer any damage as a result of relying on the incorrect certificate. On the contrary, the damage arises as a result of the buyer taking delivery without being obliged to do so, then having the vessel checked by experts and then making his own commercial decision to have her repaired. It is difficult to see why the classification society should shoulder the financial consequences to the buyer. Even if, under English law, the buyer is not entitled to refuse delivery, then the law would not permit him to claim specific performance in the sense of demanding that the seller puts right all defects in the vessel. The buyer would be restricted to a claim in damages, such damages being calculated by reference to the difference, if any, between the actual value of the vessel and the agreed purchase price.

In a recent decision the Court of Appeal in Hamburg expressed the view *obiter dictum* that, in principle, it could see the 'protective umbrella' of the contract between the seller and the classification society being extended to cover the buyer. In that case the relevant class certificate states:

> The present period of class is valid from April 1983 until April 1987, provided that the prescribed surveys are effected at their due dates. According to records available in head office of the Germanischer Lloyd the vessel is free of recommendations and average damages in respect of classification.

This certificate had expressly been issued solely on the basis of the records kept in the files of the classification society and the representations made therein were in all respects true. There could therefore be no claim for damages by the buyer. The court's observations with regard to whether such claim for damages, if there had been one, would have been contractual in nature, were therefore irrelevant for deciding this particular case.

On the other hand, the Hamburg Court of Appeal in the same decision (*MV Mayonami*) went on to set out, again *obiter*, a very interesting observation on the question as to whether or not the buyer deserved particular protection in these circumstances. The court held that, in accordance with § 334 German Civil Code, the position of the buyer is subject to all terms and defences available to the classification society against the seller. From this it follows that:

- any general terms and conditions agreed upon between the seller and the classification society are equally applicable *vis-à-vis* the buyer.
- with regard to giving due notice about defects, all responsibility rests

solely with the seller. The seller is and remains responsible *vis-à-vis* the class that any defects which might impair the class, are taken care of.

— the classification society is not liable to the buyer for any failure on the part of the seller to notify the classification society of such defects.
— notice which the classification society receives from a third party with regard to defects does not require the society to take action. In particular, it is not the job of the classification society to protect the seller against claims relating to defects of which he has not given any notice.
— the buyer has accepted under the sale contract that giving notice of defects is incumbent on the seller. The risk that the seller might not comply with this obligation cannot be shifted to the classification society.

These observations lead to the conclusion that the buyer of a ship, if he is afforded the protective umbrella of the contract between two other parties, cannot have more rights and protection than the contractual partner of the classification society. It follows that liability *vis-à-vis* the third party can be excluded in standard terms to the same extent as this is permissible *vis-à-vis* the shipowner/seller. This would adequately correspond to the role and function of the classification societies in their primary and foremost pursuit of safety aboard ships.

CHRISTIAN BREITZKE

CHAPTER 7

GERMAN PERSPECTIVE: RESPONSIBILITIES OF CLASSIFICATION SOCIETIES

For more than 70 years classification societies have had a de facto immunity status in Germany. The certificates of the German classification society, Germanischer Lloyd, as far as the jurisdiction is available, have not been the subject of a lawsuit since the Reichsgericht, in 1907, rejected a liability claim against a classification society for lack of a statutory basis for such a claim.

Throughout the intervening years, German jurisdiction has created various liability systems outside the statutory liability regulations in order to close certain gaps in the civil code. One of these constructions is the 'contract with protecting effect to third parties', a development of the contract in favour of third parties, defined in § 328 of the German Civil Code.

Based upon this jurisdiction, there have recently been incidents whereby some buyers have, after delivery of their newly purchased vessels, found them to be in a substandard condition according to the certificates issued by the classification societies. The classification societies were held liable to damages before the German courts. Although none of these procedures have ended with a judgment against the classification society to date—one case has been dismissed, another amicably settled—there appears to be a good chance that in future classification societies will no longer be untouchable but will be responsible, in financial terms, for the correctness of their statements.

The German classification society, GL, has both a public and private sphere. According to its articles of association, GL is a private company. The surveyors fulfil partly public duties, because they check upon the instructions of the Seeberufsgenossenschaft (the public insurer against accidents at work), the observance of accident-prevention and the other safety regulations with public character. They give permissions and issue certificates. This part of their work is the result of a contract concluded in 1895 between the Seeberufsgenossenschaft and GL and this is also subject to statutory law.

On the other hand GL may operate on a private basis when classifying foreign-flag vessels or other technical units or surveying repair work done on ships. These private activities are generally carried out on the instruction of the shipowner who wants to make sure that his ship complies with certain safety regulations. Such instructions from a shipowner can, in legal terms, be qualified as a contract upon conclusion of which the classification society has to give certain information as to the vessel's technical condition. The issue of a certificate is not the major subject of the contract. Rather more important is the question whether it is the supply of information or of a certificate which is owed under the contract, as the liability consequences may be different depending on whether or not the correct information is considered as a principle or a subordinate obligation.

A liability for faults in the fulfilment of public duties is not generally excluded from damage claims under German law. Such liability falls under a different category of damage claims (claims against a state body), which can only be raised by members of those states with which reciprocity in this respect is agreed on the basis of a bilateral convention.

When acting on a private basis, the classification society acts to fulfil the contractual relationship made with the shipowner who has requested the survey. Consequently, any liability claims could be raised by the shipowner who is party to the contract.

Where incorrect certificates have been issued before the sale or delivery of a vessel the buyer, who was not party to the contract with the classification society, generally has no warranty claim against the seller under the Norwegian Sales form. The German Civil Code (§ 328) recognises the contract in favour of third parties establishing a direct obligation of a contracting party to a third party. Basically, § 328 BGB is applicable for a contract between A and B where A accepts the obligation to perform (to pay, for example) to C. In the development of this rule German jurisdiction has established the 'Vertrag mit Schutzwirkung zugunsten Dritter', the contract with protective effect in favour of third parties. This construction is relevant to those contracts which are mainly concluded for the protection of a third party, though this party has no own original right of performance. A major field of application of this system is, for example, the certification of a balance sheet by a chartered accountant. The shareholder, the creditor, the purchaser of a company, the employee whose salary depends on the company's profit and also the tax authorities, are not normally party to the contract with the auditor who has received his instruction from the company's managing director on behalf of the company. They cannot enforce any such contract. The auditor's certificate is, however, issued just for those parties who do not have the knowledge of the company's financial situation. They are to be protected by the accountant's opinion, they rely on it and should have a direct claim for damages in cases where the certificate is incorrect.

In fact, since this reflects the usual situation, the accountant is fully aware of his duty towards the third party. The accountant knows, whether expressly mentioned in the contract or not, that his certificate is not only used as an internal document required by law, but as a sort of insurance for third parties against an untrue statement by the company. Under these circumstances, the situation is so close to that of a contract wherein the third party is directly mentioned and has its own right of performance (§ 328 Civil Code) that, though not directly provided by statutory law, the German jurisdiction has accepted an analogous application of the aforementioned Civil Code rule.

The situation of the classification societies is not identical but very similar: when certifying upon the instruction of a shipowner, they can generally assume that the certificate will be used as a sort of guarantee to third parties, particularly buyers of a vessel. If the classification society has concrete knowledge of a forthcoming sale there can be no doubt as to the obligation. But even if it has no such knowledge, it may be reasonable not to make any difference to the position of an auditor, particularly since classification societies themselves have taken a commercial attitude and receive a substantial remuneration from their clients. Why should they not be responsible for faults just like any other number of professions rendering services?

A breakthrough on the issue of liability claims against classification societies came on 14 June 1990. The Hamburg Court of Appeal rendered a (final) judgment of liability for a faulty certificate in a liability case against GL. The court held that a classification society which has been requested by the shipowner to confirm the class has to take into consideration that the certificate is to be presented to a third party, generally a buyer or an insurance company. It held, furthermore, that this third party trusts in the diligent and competent conduct of the survey of the classification society. In the opinion of the court, as the buyer does not generally have the expertise to examine the technical status of a ship he, as well as the direct contractual partner of the classification society, has an interest (which is to be protected) in making sure the certificate correctly reflects the result of the survey. The court stated that for this reason it seemed justified in this instance that the third party's protection of a buyer is assured in the case of the issuance of a class certificate and that the buyer was party to the sphere of protection offered by the contract between the seller and GL.

However the court did not finally accept the buyer's/plaintiff's claim for another reason: in the particular case, the defendant did not carry out a survey and issued a certificate which had been delivered to the buyer; It only repeated and referred to the content of the documents, according to which the class was in no way restricted. The confirmation expressly mentioned that it had been based upon the documents available. The classification society in this case, therefore, had only given a quasi-formal certificate on the existing class, not a statement on the actual condition of the ship.

Nevertheless, the aforementioned judgment constitutes a small revolution in the field of liabilities of classification societies under German law. There are presently several other cases pending at the Hamburg Courts in the first instance, some of which appear to have good prospects of success for the litigating buyers.

There is a special problem connected with the German law on general business terms and conditions. It may be assumed that classification societies generally try to incorporate their General Terms in the contractual relationship with their client (the selling shipowner) and that such terms contain clauses excluding liability for faults. Generally the regime of contracts in favour of third parties does not grant them more rights than those granted to the contracting party. This means that any valid exclusion of liability in the contract between the shipowner and the classification society would also affect the position of the third party.

Considering the above, the classification society could probably exclude any liability towards third parties if this were to be agreed on an individual basis. Such an exclusion of liability in the General Business Terms is, however, more difficult. The German jurisdiction distinguishes between different grades of negligence (negligence and gross negligence) and different types of obligations (major obligations and subordinate obligations). According to the General Business Terms and Conditions, an exclusion of liability for gross negligence of a major obligation is invalid. This means that any clause, whether expressly providing for such exclusion or whether providing exclusion just for any liability for faults, is invalid. Consequently, any clause excluding liability for negligence and gross negligence which fails to distinguish between the types of obligation does not sufficiently protect the classification society against liability claims of third parties or even the contracting party. This is why it is rather important to consider (and the Hamburg Court of Appeal did so) the information supplied by the classification society in order to ascertain the major obligation under the contract and not just the issuance of the certificate.

The differentiation of types of obligation appears somewhat academic but, in view of the rather important applicability of the law on General Business Terms, it can be of great importance.

Considering that the above jurisdiction will be supported by other German court decisions and confirmed by the Supreme Court, it is important to raise the question as to whether a buyer is sufficiently protected by the provisions of the commonly used (Norwegian) sale form. In clause 11 para. 2 it stipulates that the vessel is to be delivered with the present class free from recommendations. Furthermore it says that the seller has to notify the classification society of any matter which could lead to the withdrawal of the class or to the imposition of a recommendation.

According to this clause, the seller does not have to arrange for a new survey. It is fully sufficient to deliver the vessel, with all existing classification certificates (clause 8 of the Norwegian Sales form), whether or not the actual condition of the ship is in conformity with the classification rules. The exception to this is the underwater parts dry docking clause.

If the seller does not follow the obligation to inform the classification society of any matter which could lead to a withdrawal of the class, this would in theory establish liabilities of the seller in practice but this would be of very limited value. Apart from evidence problems for the buyer, it is simply impossible to get hold of the company selling its only ship or its assets the day after delivery. The classification society would refer to the correctness of the documentation at the time of the last survey and would argue that it had not been informed by the seller of any matters affecting the class. Consequently, just as the case mentioned above, there is no blame attached on the classification society which would escape from liability.

The safest solution may be to let the classification society participate in the risk and agree, in the memorandum of agreement on a survey to be held prior to delivery (not only on the underwater parts), leading to a new certificate confirming the class free of recommendations. This is sometimes agreed in sales contracts but is not subject to the standard conditions. Subsequently it is to be noted that the memorandum of agreement of the Norwegian Sales form does not provide sufficient security for the buyer. In view of the classification societies' accepting increasing responsibilities in many jurisdictions it would be a great advantage if there were provisions for a full survey of the vessel to be delivered and a new classification certificate to be provided for in the standard sales form.

The number of cases in this field of law differs greatly. There are so many variables to be taken into consideration that it is impossible to treat different cases as being more or less identical. Apart from the different legal issues, there are generally numerous factual problems to be overcome when holding the classification societies liable. This means that any judgment in this field of law can only have the character of a precedent case to a very small extent. After many years of silence things are beginning to move in this area of law in Germany; a move towards responsibility for the correctness of statements and certificates by classification societies.

CORNELIUS BRANDI

APPENDIX 1

CASE DIGEST

The 'Morning Watch'
Mariola Marine Corporation v. Lloyd's Register of Shipping

QBD (Phillips J)—15 February 1990

The plaintiff purchased the *Morning Watch*, an 80 ft steel-hulled motor yacht, in March 1985. The yacht had just been surveyed by a Lloyd's surveyor and had effectively been given a clean bill of health and classed 100A1.

The plaintiff contended that the *Morning Watch* had serious defects which rendered her unseaworthy and which should have been detected had the survey been properly conducted. The plaintiff brought proceedings against Lloyd's Register alleging negligence.

Held, that the plaintiff had established that it was reasonably foreseeable to Lloyd's that the plaintiff might rely on the survey result. But that was not in itself enough to establish a duty of care in a case of economic loss. There also had to be a sufficient degree of proximity between plaintiff and defendant, and it had to be just and reasonable to impose on the defendant a duty of care to the plaintiff.

There was no universal test to determine whether the necessary proximity existed. Under Lloyd's system of classification, parties other than the owners of classified vessels were expected to rely on the fact that a vessel was maintained in a class as providing an assurance that the vessel was maintained in good condition. But the primary purpose of the system was to enhance the safety of life and property at sea, rather than to protect the economic interests of those involved in shipping.

In so far as negligent classification was liable to harm economic interests, there was no general ground for distinguishing those of the charterer, the mortgagee or the purchaser, all of whom were at risk of this particular form of economic loss. The Court of Appeal in *Caparo Industries* v. *Dickman* [1989] QB 653 had found that a company's auditors owed a duty of care to its shareholders. Among the factors that appeared to have led the court to that decision were the statutory role of auditors, the voluntary assumption by the auditors of direct responsibility to the individual shareholders and the fact that their relationship was akin to contract.

In the present case there was no statutory scheme and no relationship akin to contract. There was no more a voluntary assumption by Lloyd's of responsibility to purchasers than there was a voluntary assumption by auditors of responsibility to potential purchasers of shares. The House of Lords had since reversed the decision of the Court of Appeal in *Caparo* v. *Dickman* and nothing in their Lordships' speeches had altered Phillips J's view of the present case.

The plaintiff's claim would be dismissed.

Belinda Bucknall QC and Luke Parsons (Ingledew Brown Bennison & Garrett) for the plaintiff; Julian Flaux (Taylor Joynson Garrett) for Lloyd's.

Editor: Michael Daiches, Barrister.

The 'Nicholas H'

QBD (Com Ct) (Hirst J)—2 July 1992

The vessel *Nicholas H* was on a laden voyage from South America to Italy when she was found to have cracks in her hull. She anchored off San Juan, Puerto Rico. Arrangements were made for her classification society, Nippon Kaiji Kyokai ('NKK'), to survey the vessel at anchor. The surveyor recommended that repairs be carried out at the nearest port prior to sailing to Italy, and that the vessel be retained as classed subject to those conditions. The recommendation would have involved permanent repairs, for which facilities were available locally.

The shipowners baulked at carrying out the recommended permanent repairs and only temporary repairs were in the event carried out. The vessel was surveyed again. The surveyor recommended that the vessel proceed to Italy, the repairs to be examined and dealt with as necessary after discharging cargo.

The vessel sailed for Italy, but on the following day the temporary repairs cracked. A few days later she sank with all her cargo.

The cargo owners brought proceedings against NKK in tort alleging that NKK were negligent in altering the initial recommendation and permitting the vessel to continue her voyage when only temporary repairs had been carried out.

A preliminary issue was held as to whether NKK owed a duty of care to the cargo owners capable of giving rise to a liability in damages.

The cargo owners submitted that there was now a clear dividing line between physical damage cases and economic loss cases. In physical damage cases all the plaintiff needed to do to establish a duty of care was to prove (i) foreseeability that lack of care might result in harm; and (ii) ownership or appropriate possessory interest in the property physically damaged or lost. There was no need to make good the two additional criteria which applied in economic loss cases, namely (iii) proximity and (iv) that it would be 'fair, just and reasonable' to impose a duty of care in tort. The cargo owners submitted that if they were wrong on their main submission, they could make good their case on (iii) and (iv) on the assumed facts.

NKK contended *inter alia* that the general principles stated in economic loss cases were equally applicable to physical damage cases, and that (iii) and (iv) applied.

Held, that the authorities showed clearly that the law had in recent years tended to draw an ever stronger contrast between economic loss and physical loss cases. However, it was not accepted that just because general statements of principle appeared in economic loss cases they invariably had to be restricted to that class.

So far as proximity was concerned it was clear that in the great majority of physical damage cases the duty of care did not give rise to any problem because it was self-evident that a duty existed (e.g. in road and factory accident cases). But, it seemed clear that proximity was a relevant criterion in physical damage cases, particularly where there was no direct physical contact between the plaintiff and defendant or between vehicles or equipment under their control.

The proximity criterion was essential in the present case, particularly since there was such a wide variety of circumstances where a party not in contractual relationship with NKK might seek to establish liability and where proximity provided a valuable test for separating the sheep from the goats.

The 'fair, just and reasonable' criterion would be relevant very exceptionally in physical damage cases, and then only if the defendants could establish that public policy considerations required the court to give immunity from a duty of care which would otherwise have been upheld.

On the assumed facts of the present case there was a very close degree of proximity between the surveyor and the cargo owners. Although the surveyor had no direct physical control over the vessel, the decisive influence on the shipowners which his second recommendations must have had, and would reasonably be foreseen to have had, was very akin to control. Therefore, on the assumed facts, a sufficiently close and direct relationship of proximity was established.

There were no special public policy considerations which justified application of the 'fair, just and reasonable' criterion. If, however, that was wrong, the court was satisfied that there was nothing on public policy grounds to debar the cargo owners from making good the duty of care.

On the facts pleaded, NKK did owe the cargo owners a duty of care *capable* of giving rise to a liability in damages. The word 'capable' was emphasised because nothing in the judgment should be interpreted as establishing that NKK actually owed such a duty of care. The assumed facts were in issue and could only be determined on a full trial after all the evidence had been heard.

Peter Gross QC (Lovell White Durrant) for the cargo owners; Richard Aikens QC and Jonathan Harvie (Norton Rose) for NKK.

Editor: Michael Daiches, Barrister.

East River SS v. TransAmerica Delaval

USA Supreme Court (Blackmun J. delivered the unanimous opinion of the Court)—1986

The plaintiff chartered one of a series of vessels which had been constructed by a shipbuilder who contracted with the defendant to design and supervise the installation of the turbines forming the main propulsion units for the vessels. The turbines malfunctioned due to design and manufacturing defects. But only the turbines themselves were damaged.

The plaintiff alleged tortious conduct based on a products-liability theory and sought damages from the defendant for the cost of repairs and income lost while the vessels were out of service.

The Federal District Court granted summary judgment for the defendant. The Court of Appeals affirmed the decision. The plaintiff appealed to the Supreme Court.

Held, that whether stated in negligence or strict liability, no products-liability claim lies in Admiralty when a commercial party alleges injury only to the product itself resulting in purely economic loss. Such a claim is most naturally a warranty claim.

This case required the court to consider first, whether Admiralty law incorporates principles of products-liability, including strict liability, and then whether injury to a product itself is the kind of harm that should be protected by principles of products-liability.

The US courts have developed a body of maritime tort principles which now clearly recognise that products-liability, including strict liability, is part of the general maritime law. The rationale in those cases, that strict liability should be imposed on the party best able to protect persons from hazardous equipment, is equally applicable when the claims are based on products-liability as when they are based on the unseaworthiness of the vessel or the failure to perform services in a workmanlike manner.

Products-liability grew out of a public policy judgment that people need more protection from dangerous products than is afforded by the law of warranty. In this case, it must be determined whether a commercial product, injuring itself, is the kind of harm which public policy requires manufacturers to be responsible for, independent of any contractual obligations.

Authority has established that products-liability covers cases where both life and limb and property are at risk. In this case, the only property damaged was the turbines themselves. To hold that there was 'property damaged' in each case where a product damages itself 'would eliminate the distinction between warranty and strict products-liability', *Northern Power and Engineering Corp* v. *Caterpillar Tractor Company*, 623 P 2d 324, 330 (Alaska 1981). When harm occurs to the product itself, the resulting loss in terms of repair costs, decreased value, and lost profits is essentially the failure of the purchaser to receive the benefit of its bargain. This is traditionally the concern of contract law.

Other factors which support this view are the built-in limitation on the damages capable of being awarded. Consequential damages must be a foreseeable result of the breach *Hadley* v. *Baxendale*. To permit recovery for all the foreseeable claims for purely economic loss could make a manufacturer liable for vast sums. In addition the losses likely to be suffered can be insured against. Alternatively, if the customer prefers it can reject the product and sue for breach of contract. In return, the manufacturer can restrict its liability within certain limits, by disclaiming warranties or limiting remedies. Since a commercial situation generally does not involve large disparative bargaining power there is no reason to intrude into the party's allocation of the risk.

In this case, the contractual responsibilities were clearly laid out and there is no reason to extricate the parties from their bargain. A manufacturer in a commercial relationship has no duty under either a negligence or strict products-liability theory to prevent a product from injuring itself.

The plaintiff's appeal will be dismissed.

Thomas E. Durkin Junior for the plaintiff; Robert E. Smith for the defendant.

Editor: Gillian Bentley, Ince & Co.

The 'Tradeways II'
Great American Insurance Company, et al v. Bureau Veritas

US District Court, Southern District of New York (Harold R. Tyler Jr DJ)—22 February 1972

The plaintiffs were the insurers of the owners and charterers of the liberty ship *Tradeways II* which sank on a voyage from Antwerp to the Great Lakes. The defendant, the ship's classification society, surveyed the *Tradeways II* first, during a routine annual survey after which they confirmed the vessel maintained her class and secondly, to perform an 'on-hire' survey for the charterers which revealed numerous defects not detected in the annual survey which resulted in the withdrawal of the classification certificate. Once certain recommended repairs had been carried out, the vessel's class was restored by the defendant.

The plaintiffs settled the various claims against owners and charterers and sought, by subrogation, an indemnity from the defendant alleging that the services rendered by the defendant were performed either negligently, or in breach of the defendant's implied warranty of workmanlike service, thereby leading to the sinking of the vessel.

The trial was limited to the issue of liability.

Held, that the plaintiffs had failed to prove (1) that the alleged breach of duty was the proximate cause of the sinking (2) that there were in fact breaches of duty, or (3) that the principles of either tort or contract law entitled them to recover.

Despite holding that the plaintiffs had failed to prove causation or negligence, the court considered the ultimate issue of the tortious or contractual liability of a classification society.

In tort, the obvious question was what duties were owed by a classification society to its clientele? By surveying and classifying a vessel a classification society was obliged to perform two duties with due care (1) to survey and classify vessels in accordance with the rules and standards established by the society for that purpose; and (2) to detect and notify the owners and charterers of any defects in the ship.

Although there was no authority on the subject, there was a long-standing policy that the owner of a ship has a non-delegable duty to maintain a seaworthy vessel. In recognition of this, the Court of Appeals has held that an owner cannot rely upon a favourable survey or classification to establish a defence of due diligence even where a classification society has certified a vessel in contravention of its own rules (*The 'Marine Sulphur'* 1970 AMC 1031). This maintains the accountability of owners for the seaworthiness of their vessels and creates a potentially insuperable bar to any recovery for breach of the classification society's first duty to survey and classify vessels in accordance with its own rules.

The court noted that despite the benefit to shipowners, ship operators and seamen, there were several undesirable effects of allowing recovery against classification societies in tort. Any liability would be disproportionate to the amount of control a classification society had over a vessel which it sees briefly once a year and would not be in accord with the parties' intentions, the fees charged or the services performed. Consequently, the second duty, to detect and warn of hazards provides a sounder basis for the tortious liability of classification societies.

In *The 'Gyda'* the court found that the defendant classification society had breached its express undertaking in an 'on-hire' survey by failing to advise the charterer it was unsafe to sail. The judgment was expressed in terms of a breach of an undertaking, but the extensive use of negligence language and tortious theories of causation suggest that had there not been a break in the chain of causation (the charterers subsequently became aware of the unsafe condition of the vessel and failed to remedy the hazard) the court would have held the classification society liable based on a breach of duty of care to detect and notify defects in the ship, as much as on a breach of contract.

In considering the possibility of contractual liability the court decided that classification societies should not be subject to the doctrine established in *Ryan Stevedoring Co* v. *Pan Atlantic Corp* (in which a stevedore was held liable for the unseaworthy condition of the vessel brought about by the un-workmanlike manner of his services). Although in agreeing to survey and classify ships classification societies contractually undertake to provide services and it was foreseeable that a failure to perform those services in a competent manner may expose owners to a risk of loss, foreseeability alone was not sufficient to establish liability. The burden of furnishing a seaworthy vessel remains that of the owner and there must be good reason to shift that burden on to another party such as a classification society.

An important factor in the distinction between the stevedores in *Ryan* and classification societies was the element of control over the dangerous condition of the vessel. As the Court of Appeals has held, if a vessel is in an unseaworthy condition which 'workmanlike service' would detect and correct, the contractor is liable for a failure to eliminate the hazard to the vessel (*DeGioia* v. *United States Lines Co* 1962 AMC 1747). It would be rare for a classification society to create hazards or defects in the 'workmanlike service' of performing its functions and activities; all a society can do is detect and report such defects. The rectification of those defects is the owners' responsibility. In addition, the broad scope of a classification society's services is such that if the *Ryan* doctrine were to apply this would produce the unwanted result of making classification societies the absolute guarantors of the vessels which they survey.

To apply the *Ryan* doctrine to a classification society would unsoundly and unfairly dilute the owners' legal duty to furnish a seaworthy vessel.

The plaintiffs' claims should be dismissed.

William A. Williams and Walter A. Hopkins (Wilson & Hopkins) for owners and their insurers; Charles S. Haight (Haight Gardner, Poor and Havens) for the remaining plaintiffs; Edwin Longcope and John F. X. McKiernan (Hill, Betts & Nash) for the defendant.

Editor: Gillian Bentley, Ince & Co.

Re The 'Amoco Cadiz'
In re oil spill by the Amoco Cadiz off the coast of France on 16 March 1978

US District Court, Northern District of Illinois (Eastern Division)—(Frank J. McGarr DJ—11 February and 15 April 1986

By Memorandum Opinion and Order dated 18 April 1984, this court found Amoco liable for the damage caused by the oil spill from the *Amoco Cadiz* because it negligently failed to ensure that the vessel was seaworthy.

The plaintiff (American Bureau of Shipping ('ABS')) was originally named as a defendant in that hearing. The plaintiff has now filed an action to recover its litigation costs and Amoco have counterclaimed that ABS is liable to indemnify them for all, or contribute to the losses incurred by them.

The court heard the plaintiff's and Amoco's cross-motions for partial summary judgment with respect to Amoco's claims for indemnity and contribution from ABS.

Held, ABS's motion for partial summary judgment with respect to Amoco's claim for indemnity was granted, but was denied with respect to Amoco's claim for contribution. Amoco's motions were also denied.

Although ABS was not represented at the trial, the Memorandum Opinion made several findings of fact which concerned ABS. ABS's involvement with the *Amoco Cadiz* included services in two distinct areas: (1) the design and construction of the vessel, and (2) periodic surveys of the vessel after it began operations. The nature and extent of those duties were the subject of the present dispute.

There were issues of fact concerning the nature of ABS's role in the design and construction of the vessel, namely whether it was limited to certifying that the design and construction were in compliance with the rules, or that the plans and construction were done properly. Similarly, there remained issues of fact regarding the exact scope of the duties of ABS in periodically surveying the vessel and whether ABS had fulfilled those duties. Despite these outstanding issues, the court considered, in principle, Amoco's claims for indemnity and contribution.

Amoco contends that it is entitled to indemnity not in tort but in contract under the doctrine in *Ryan Stevedoring Co* v. *Atlantic Steamship Corp*, 350 US 124, 1956 AMC 9 (1956). In *Ryan*, the Supreme Court held a shipowner could recover damages paid to a longshoreman from a stevedore who had breached his warranty of workmanlike service in unsafely stowing the cargo which caused the victim's injuries. However, in this case the evidence showed that ABS did not agree to assume all liability in the event of the ship's failure, nor were there any special circumstances regarding the relationship between ABS and Amoco to indicate Amoco should be entitled to indemnity. Moreover, in this case, the oil spill was due to the shipbuilders' negligence in designing or constructing the ship. There was also negligence on the part of Amoco in failing to fulfil its obligation to maintain the seaworthiness of the vessel. Consequently, Amoco is not being held liable for an incident due solely to the negligence of another and the doctrine in *Ryan* shold not apply. The nature of an indemnity claim is to transfer the whole liability to another and therefore Amoco's claim for an indemnity must fail.

Amoco's claim for a contribution alleges that ABS was concurrently negligent in failing to detect defects during its periodic surveys. ABS contends that it cannot be held liable to third parties under Section 324A of the Restatement (Second) of Tort because its failure, if any, to exercise reasonable care did not increase the risk of harm.

In *Patentas* v. *United States* it was held that a party is not deemed to have increased the risk of harm in the absence of some physical change to the environment or some material alteration of the circumstances. The failure to detect already existing defects cannot be said to increase the risk in any real or logical manner. However Amoco alleges that ABS's duty went beyond merely detecting existing defects. Amoco argues that in approving the plans for the vessel, ABS had a certain amount of control over the design of the ship which goes beyond merely inspecting plans which already exist. Due to these outstanding factual issues regarding the nature of ABS's involvement and role in the design and construction of the vessel, in addition to questions of fact as to the reliance, if any, by Amoco upon ABS's undertaking when Amoco had knowledge of the dangerous conditions on its vessel, ABS is not entitled to summary judgment on the question of Amoco's claim for contribution.

Frank T Cicero Jr, PC, Roger L Taylor and Jonathan B Newcomb (Kirkland and Ellis) and James T Stuhlreder (Amoco Corporation) for Amoco parties; John D Gordon, III and Monica Derham (Lord Day and Lord) and Gerard G Saltarelli and Robert S Hermes (Butler Rubin, Newcomer Saltarelli and Boyd) for ABS.

The 'Hecht V'
A claim against Germanischer Lloyd

Hanseatisches Oberlandesgericht (Court of Appeal), Hamburg—14 June 1990

The plaintiff was the legal successor of the buyer of the *Hecht V* which was sold to the buyer on 8 April 1986 'with present Class free of recommendations'.

The defendant surveyed certain repairs done to the vessel and issued a certificate stating: 'According to the records available in the Head Office of Germanischer Lloyd the vessel is free of recommendation and average damages in respect of Classification.' The defendant did not change its position despite the buyer pointing out serious defects which remained in the vessel.

After delivery, the buyer's classification society (Bureau Veritas) surveyed the vessel and required the defects to be remedied.

The seller having gone bankrupt, the plaintiff brought proceedings against the defendant claiming to be 'protected' by the benefit of the survey contract between the seller and the defendant.

Held, that the authorities show that protective liabilities can result from a contractual obligation in favour of third parties who are not entitled to the performance of the contract. This has become known as a 'contract with protective effect for the benefit of third parties'.

If the contracting parties do not expressly provide for the third party to be benefited, contractual liability must only be extended towards third parties where it is reasonable to do so.

To establish the 'protective effect' it must be shown that:

- the third party's position is affected by the services rendered;
- that the obligee (in this case the seller) has a special interest in the protection of third parties;
- that both these elements are known to the obligor (in this case the defendant classification society); and
- that the third party is in need of protection.

It is questionable whether the seller of a vessel has a special interest in the protection of buyers. This element of personal care in the relationship between the obligee and the third party is not a *sine qua non* for the 'protective effect' to be established but where it does exist, the 'protective effect' and the intention to benefit the third party can be assumed.

In this case, the court considered that the necessary conditions had been fulfilled to establish that the buyer (and now the plaintiff) was entitled to the benefit of the 'protective effect' of the contract between the seller and the defendant.

There is wide authority to support the case that contracts involving the preparation of expert opinions, or providing information, give 'protective effect' to third parties if the opinion or information will obviously be made available to the third party. If such an opinion or information is incorrect, the third party who suffers loss as a result of relying upon the correctness of the opinion is entitled to damages.

When buying a vessel, great importance is attached by the buyer to the class of the vessel. Consequently, a classification society requested to issue a confirmation of class by the owner must expect that the certificate will be submitted to a third party who will rely upon the correctness of its content. The classification society must also expect that the third party will rely upon the surveys performed being done carefully and competently. The buyer is not in a position to evaluate the vessel's condition and his interest is as worthy of protection as that of the direct contractual party to the contract with the classification society. Thus, the buyer of a vessel is entitled to the protection of the contract between the classification society and the seller.

In this case, however, the certificate issued was formally correct as it reflected the contents of the files in the defendant's possession and was issued on no other basis.

The plaintiff's claim was therefore dismissed.

Editors: Cornelius Brandi, Weiss & Hasche; Gillian Bentley, Ince & Co.

APPENDIX 2

LLOYD'S REGISTER SPECIMEN FORMS

FLEET SERVICES DEPARTMENT CERTIFICATES

Lloyd's Register of Shipping

REQUEST FOR STATUTORY APPROVALS AND FOR ISSUE OF CERTIFICATES FOR EXISTING L.R. CLASS SHIPS

Ship's Name

L.R. No.

Flag

This ship is classed by Lloyd's Register of Shipping with the notation and it is our intention to maintain this classification.

We request that the following certificates be issued and documents approved by Lloyd's Register of Shipping for which we agree to pay the Society's fees and any expenses or a pro rata charge in the event of the documentation not being required by us.

Certificates

Load Line & SOLAS		Tonnage		Other		
Load Line	☐	National	☐	Cargo Gear	☐	☐
Passenger Safety	☐	British (Non-UK ships)	☐		☐	☐
Safety Construction	☐	Canadian Appendix	☐		☐	☐
Safety Equipment	☐	Suez Canal	☐		☐	☐
Radiotelegraphy	☐	Panama Canal	☐		☐	☐
Radiotelephony	☐		☐		☐	☐

Approvals

Stability Information	☐	Grain Loading	☐	Crew Accommodation (Specify Rules)	☐	☐

For LR local office use

Office:

Owner's Stamp and Signature

Form 2547 Req 3 (2/80)

COPY

Lloyd's Register of Shipping

REQUEST FOR THE
CLASSIFICATION OR RE-CLASSIFICATION OF AN EXISTING SHIP
PLEASE SUBMIT IN DUPLICATE TO YOUR LOCAL L.R. OFFICE

NAME OF SHIP		L.R. NUMBER	DATE OF BUILD
BUILDER		PROPOSED REGISTRY	
	YARD NO.	TYPE OF SHIP	
OWNER		CLASS AND NOTATIONS REQUIRED – (HULL, MACHINERY, REFRIGERATION, UMS, IGS OR ICE CLASS)	
TYPE OF ENGINE			
MANUFACTURER OF ENGINE			
THE SHIP IS PRESENTLY CLASSED WITH		AND HAS THE FOLLOWING NOTATIONS	

We hereby authorise Lloyd's Register of Shipping to request from the above mentioned Society, in accordance with the IACS Agreement, to provide an up-to-date survey status report.

We request that the above vessel be surveyed by Lloyd's Register of Shipping for classification and agree to pay the Survey Fee and any variation therefrom which has been notified and any travelling and other expenses which may be incurred by the Surveyors in connection with the survey. In the event of the survey not being proceeded with we agree to pay on a *pro-rata* basis for the services provided.

In addition, we request that the following certificates be issued and documents approved by Lloyd's Register of Shipping for which we agree to pay the Society's fees and any expenses on a *pro-rata* charge in the event of the documentation not being required by us.

CERTIFICATES

LOAD LINE AND SOLAS	TONNAGE	OTHER	OTHER
LOAD LINE ☐	NATIONAL ☐	CARGO GEAR ☐	☐
PASSENGER SAFETY ☐	BRITISH (NON-UK) SHIPS ☐	MARPOL ☐	☐
SAFETY CONSTRUCTION ☐	CANADIAN APPENDIX ☐	CHEMICAL CODE ☐	☐
SAFETY EQUIPMENT ☐	SUEZ CANAL ☐	GAS CODE ☐	☐
RADIOTELEGRAPHY ☐	PANAMA CANAL ☐	☐	☐
RADIOTELEPHONY ☐	☐	☐	☐

APPROVALS

STABILITY INFORMATION ☐	GRAIN LOADING ☐	CREW ACCOMMODATION (SPECIFY RULES)* ☐	☐

*RULES

OWNER'S STAMP AND SIGNATURE

DATE

In providing services information or advice neither the Society nor any of its servants or agents warrants the accuracy of any information or advice supplied. Except as set out herein neither the Society nor any of its servants or agents (on behalf of each of whom the Society has agreed this clause) shall be liable for any loss damage or expense whatever sustained by any person due to any act or omission or error of whatsoever nature and howsoever caused of the Society its servants or agents or due to any inaccuracy of whatsoever nature and howsoever caused in any information or advice given in any way whatsoever by or on behalf of the Society, even if held to amount to a breach of warranty. Nevertheless, if any person uses the Society's services or relies on any information or advice given by or on behalf of the Society and suffers loss damage or expense thereby which is proved to have been due to any negligent act omission or error of the Society its servants or agents or any negligent inaccuracy in information or advice given by or on behalf of the Society then the Society will pay compensation to such person for his proved loss up to but not exceeding the amount of the fee (if any) charged by the Society for that particular service information or advice.

Form 2548 (RI)

Lloyd's Register

CERTIFICATE OF CLASS

This is to certify that the

Lloyd's Register Number

Built by

At

Date of Build

Registered Tonnages:

Gross Net

having been surveyed by the Society's Surveyors and reported by them to be in a fit and efficient condition in accordance with the Rules and Regulations of Lloyd's Register of Shipping, has been assigned the class:

Chairman

Secretary

Date of Issue

Lloyd's Register of Shipping
71 Fenchurch Street, London EC3M 4BS

NOTICE—This certificate is subject to the Terms and Conditions overleaf, which form part of this certificate.

TERMS AND CONDITIONS

Continuance of Class is subject to compliance with the requirements of the Society's Rules and Regulations.

In providing services information or advice neither the Society nor any of its servants or agents warrants the accuracy of any information or advice supplied. Except as set out herein neither the Society nor any of its servants or agents (on behalf of each of whom the Society has agreed this clause) shall be liable for any loss damage or expense whatever sustained by any person due to any act or omission or error of whatsoever nature and howsoever caused of the Society its servants or agents or due to any inaccuracy of whatsoever nature and howsoever caused in any information or advice given in any way whatsoever by or on behalf of the Society, even if held to amount to a breach of warranty. Nevertheless, if any person uses the Society's services or relies on any information or advice given by or on behalf of the Society and suffers loss damage or expense thereby which is proved to have been due to any negligent act omission or error of the Society its servants or agents or any negligent inaccuracy in information or advice given by or on behalf of the Society then the Society will pay compensation to such person for his proved loss up to but not exceeding the amount of the fee (if any) charged by the Society for that particular service information or advice.

The Society, its officers servants and agents (on behalf of whom this notice is given) shall be under no liability or responsibility in negligence or otherwise howsoever to any person who is not a party to the agreement pursuant to which this certificate is issued in respect of any information or advice expressly or impliedly given by or in this certificate or in respect of any omission or inaccuracy herein or in respect of any act or omission which has caused or contributed to this certificate being issued with the information and advice it contains (if any).

Nº:
Page 1 of 1

Lloyd's Register

Cargo Ship Safety Radio Certificate

This Certificate shall be supplemented by a Record of Equipment of Radio Facilities (Form R), Nº:

Issued under the provisions of the International Convention for the Safety of Life at Sea, 1974, as amended (hereinafter referred to as 'the Convention') under the authority of the Government of

Particulars of Ship

Name of ship

Distinctive number or letters

Port of registry

Gross tonnage

Sea areas in which ship is certified to operate (regulation IV/2)

IMO Number

Date on which keel was laid[1]

SPECIMEN

This is to certify:

1. that the ship has been surveyed in accordance with the requirements of regulation I/9 of the Convention;
2. that the survey showed that:
   - 2.1 the ship complied with the requirements of the Convention as regards radio installations;
   - 2.2 the functioning of the radio installations used in life-saving appliances complied with the requirements of the Convention;
3. that an Exemption Certificate has / has not[2] been issued.

This certificate is valid until

Issued at on

The undersigned declares that Lloyd's Register of Shipping is duly authorised by the said Government to issue this certificate.

Lloyd's Register of Shipping
71 Fenchurch Street, London EC3M 4BS

[1] Date on which keel was laid or ship was at a similar stage of construction or, where applicable, date on which work for a conversion or an alteration or modification of a major character was commenced.
[2] Delete as appropriate.

FORM 1705 (11/91) 1/1

Record Nº
Page 1 of 2

Record of Equipment for the Cargo Ship Safety Radio Certificate (FORM R)

This Record shall be permanently attached to the Cargo Ship Safety Radio Certificate

Record of Equipment of Radio Facilities for compliance with the International Convention for the Safety of Life at Sea, 1974, as amended in 1988

1. PARTICULARS OF SHIP

Name of ship	
Distinctive number or letters	IMO number
Minimum number of persons with required qualifications to operate the radio installations	

2. DETAILS OF RADIO FACILITIES

ITEM	ACTUAL PROVISION
2.1 Primary systems	
2.1.1 VHF radio installation	
2.1.1.1 DSC encoder	
2.1.1.2 DSC watch receiver	
2.1.1.3 Radiotelephony	
2.1.2 MF radio installation	
2.1.2.1 DSC encoder	
2.1.2.2 DSC watch receiver	
2.1.2.3 Radiotelephony	
2.1.3 MF/HF radio installation	
2.1.3.1 DSC encoder	
2.1.3.2 DSC watch receiver	
2.1.3.3 Radiotelephony	
2.1.3.4 Direct-printing telegraphy	
2.1.4 INMARSAT ship earth station	
2.2 Secondary means of alerting	
2.3 Facilities for reception of maritime safety information	
2.3.1 NAVTEX receiver	
2.3.2 EGC receiver	
2.3.3 HF direct-printing radiotelegraph receiver	
2.4 Satellite EPIRB	
2.4.1 COSPAS-SARSAT	
2.4.2 INMARSAT	

FORM 2131 (10/91) 1/2

Record Nº
Page 2 of 2

2. DETAILS OF RADIO FACILITIES - CONTINUED

ITEM	ACTUAL PROVISION
2.5 VHF EPIRB	
2.6 Ship's radar transponder	
2.7 Radiotelephone distress frequency watch receiver on 2,182 kHz	
2.8 Device for generating the radiotelephone alarm signal on 2,182 kHz	

3. METHODS USED TO ENSURE AVAILABILITY OF RADIO FACILITIES (regulations IV/15.6 and 15.7)

3.1 Duplication of equipment	
3.2 Shore-based maintenance	
3.3 At-sea maintenance capability	

4. SHIPS CONSTRUCTED BEFORE 1 FEBRUARY 1995 WHICH DO NOT COMPLY WITH ALL THE APPLICABLE REQUIREMENTS OF CHAPTER IV OF THE CONVENTION AS AMENDED IN 1988

4.1 For ships required to be fitted with radiotelegraphy in accordance with the Convention in force prior to 1 February 1992

	REQUIREMENTS OF REGULATIONS	ACTUAL PROVISION
Hours of listening by operator		
Number of operators		
Whether auto alarm fitted		
Whether main installation fitted		
Whether reserve installation fitted		
Whether main and reserve transmitters electrically separated or combined		

4.2 For ships required to be fitted with radiotelephony in accordance with the Convention in force prior to 1 February 1992

	REQUIREMENTS OF REGULATIONS	ACTUAL PROVISION
Hours of listening		
Number of operators		

This is to certify that, on the date of issue, this Record was correct in all respects.

Issued at

on

Lloyd's Register of Shipping
71 Fenchurch Street, London EC3M 4BS

FORM 2131 (10/91) 2/2

Nº:
Page 1 of 2

Lloyd's Register

Cargo Ship Safety Equipment Certificate

This Certificate shall be supplemented by a Record of Equipment (Form E), Nº

Issued under the provisions of the International Convention for the Safety of Life at Sea, 1974, as amended, and as modified by the Protocol of 1978 relating thereto (hereinafter referred to as 'the Convention') under the authority of the Government of

Particulars of Ship

Name of ship

Distinctive number or letters

Port of registry

Gross tonnage

Deadweight of ship (metric tons)[1]

Length of ship (regulation III/3.10)

IMO Number

Type of Ship: Oil tanker[2] / Chemical tanker[2] / Gas carrier[2] / Cargo ship other than any of the above[2]

Date on which keel was laid[3]

This is to certify:

1. that the ship has been surveyed in accordance with the requirements of regulation I/8 of the Convention as modified by the 1978 Protocol relating thereto;
2. that the survey showed that:
   - 2.1 the ship complied with the requirements of the Convention as regards fire safety systems and appliances and fire control plans;
   - 2.2 the life-saving appliances and the equipment of the lifeboats, liferafts and rescue boats were provided in accordance with the requirements of the Convention;
   - 2.3 the ship was provided with a line-throwing appliance and radio installations used in life-saving appliances in accordance with the requirements of the Convention;
   - 2.4 the ship complied with the requirements of the Convention as regards shipborne navigational equipment, nautical publications and means of embarkation for pilots;
   - 2.5 the ship was provided with lights, shapes, means of making sound signals and distress signals in accordance with the requirements of the Convention and the International Regulations for Preventing Collisions at Sea in force;
   - 2.6 in all other respects the ship complied with the relevant requirements of the Convention;

[1] For Oil tankers/Chemical tankers and Gas carriers only. [2] Delete as appropriate.
[3] Date on which keel was laid or ship was at a similar stage of construction or, where applicable, date on which work for a conversion or an alteration or modification of a major character was commenced.

FORM 1703 (11/91) 1/2

Nº:
Page 2 of 2

3. that the ship operates in accordance with regulation III/26.1.1.1 within the limits of the trade area:

4. that in implementing regulation I/6(b) the Government has instituted mandatory annual surveys;

5. that an Exemption Certificate has / has not[2] been issued;

6. that a Lloyd's Register of Shipping Document of Compliance in accordance with regulation 54 of chapter II-2 for ships carrying dangerous goods has/has not[2] been issued.

This certificate is valid until

Issued at on

The undersigned declares that Lloyd's Register of Shipping is duly authorised by the said Government to issue this certificate.

Lloyd's Register of Shipping
71 Fenchurch Street, London EC3M 4BS

Mandatory annual survey

This is to certify that the ship has been surveyed in accordance with regulation I/6(b) of the Convention, as modified by the 1978 Protocol and the relevant recommendations of the Organisation.

Mandatory annual survey[5] *Date*

Place of survey *Surveyor to Lloyd's Register of Shipping*

Intermediate survey for tankers of 10 years of age and over

This is to certify that, at an intermediate survey required by regulation I/8 of the Convention, as modified by the 1978 Protocol, this ship was found to comply with the relevant provisions of the Convention[4].

Intermediate survey *Date*

Place of survey *Surveyor to Lloyd's Register of Shipping*

Under the provisions of regulation I/14 of the Convention, as modified by the 1978 Protocol, the validity of this Certificate is extended until

Date

Place of survey *Surveyor to Lloyd's Register of Shipping*

[2] Delete as appropriate.
[4] Reference is made to the Guidelines on surveys required by the 1978 SOLAS Protocol, the International Bulk Chemical Code and the International Gas Carrier Code adopted by the Organisation by resolution A.560(14).
[5] An intermediate survey may take the place of a mandatory annual survey.

FORM 1703 (11/91) 2/2

Record Nº
Page 1 of 2

Record of Equipment for the Cargo Ship Safety Equipment Certificate (FORM E)

This Record shall be permanently attached to the Cargo Ship Safety Equipment Certificate

Record of Equipment for compliance with the International Convention for the Safety of Life at Sea, 1974, as amended in 1988

1. PARTICULARS OF SHIP

Name of ship	
Distinctive number or letters	IMO number

2. DETAILS OF LIFE-SAVING APPLIANCES

2.1 Total number of persons for which life-saving appliances are provided		
	PORT SIDE	STARBOARD SIDE
2.2 Total number of lifeboats		
2.2.1 Total number of persons accommodated by them		
2.2.2 Number of self-righting partially enclosed lifeboats (regulation III/43)		
2.2.3 Number of totally enclosed lifeboats (regulation III/44)		
2.2.4 Number of lifeboats with a self-contained air support system (regulation III/45)		
2.2.5 Number of fire-protected lifeboats (regulation III/46)		
2.2.6 Other lifeboats		
2.2.6.1 Number		
2.2.6.2 Type		
2.2.7 Number of freefall lifeboats		
2.2.7.1 Totally enclosed (regulation III/44)		
2.2.7.2 Self-contained (regulation III/45)		
2.2.7.3 Fire-protected (regulation III/46)		

2.3 Number of motor lifeboats (included in the total lifeboats shown above)	
2.3.1 Number of motor lifeboats fitted with searchlights	
2.4 Number of rescue boats	
2.4.1 Number of rescue boats which are included in the total lifeboats shown above	
2.5 Liferafts	
2.5.1 Liferafts for which approved launching appliances are required	
2.5.1.1 Number of liferafts	
2.5.1.2 Number of persons accommodated by them	

FORM 2130 (10/91) 1/2

Record Nº
Page 2 of 2

2. DETAILS OF LIFE-SAVING APPLIANCES (CONTINUED)

2.5.2 Liferafts for which approved launching appliances are not required	
2.5.2.1 Number of liferafts	
2.5.2.2 Number of persons accommodated by them	
2.5.3 Number of liferafts required by regulation III/26.1.4	
2.6 Number of lifebuoys	
2.7 Number of lifejackets	
2.8 Immersion suits	
2.8.1 Total number of immersion suits	
2.8.2 Number of suits complying with the requirements for lifejackets	
2.9 Number of thermal protective aids[1]	
2.10 Radio installations used in life-saving appliances	
2.10.1 Number of radar transponders	
2.10.2 Number of two-way VHF radiotelephone apparatus	

3. SHIPS CONSTRUCTED BEFORE 1 FEBRUARY 1992 WHICH DO NOT FULLY COMPLY WITH THE APPLICABLE REQUIREMENTS OF CHAPTER III OF THE CONVENTION AS AMENDED IN 1988

	ACTUAL PROVISION
Radiotelegraph installation for lifeboat	
Portable radio apparatus for survival craft	
Survival craft EPIRB (121.5 MHz and 243.0 MHz)	
Two-way radiotelephone apparatus	

This is to certify that, on the date of issue, this Record was correct in all respects.

Issued at

on

Lloyd's Register of Shipping
71 Fenchurch Street, London EC3M 4BS

FORM 2130 (10/91) 2/2

[1] Excluding those required by regulations III/38.5.1.24, III/41.8.31 and III/47.2.2.13

Nº:
Page 1 of 2

Lloyd's Register

Cargo Ship Safety Construction Certificate

Issued under the provisions of the International Convention for the Safety of Life at Sea, 1974, as amended, and as modified by the Protocol of 1978 relating thereto (hereinafter referred to as 'the Convention') under the authority of the Government of

Particulars of Ship

Name of ship

Distinctive number or letters

Port of registry

Gross tonnage

Deadweight of ship (metric tons)[1]

IMO Number

Type of Ship: Oil tanker[2] / Chemical tanker[2] / Gas carrier[2] / Cargo ship other than any of the above[2]

Date on which keel was laid[3]

This is to certify:

1. that the ship has been surveyed in accordance with the requirements of regulation I/10 of the Convention as modified by the 1978 Protocol;
2. that the survey showed that the condition of the structure, machinery and equipment as defined in the above regulation was satisfactory and the ship complied with the relevant requirements of chapters II-1 and II-2 of the Convention (other than those relating to fire safety systems and appliances and fire control plans);
3. that in implementing regulation I/6(b) the Government has instituted mandatory annual surveys;
4. that an Exemption Certificate has / has not[2] been issued;
5. that a Lloyd's Register of Shipping Document of Compliance in accordance with regulation 54 of chapter II-2 for ships carrying dangerous goods has/has not[2] been issued.

This certificate is valid until

Issued at on

The undersigned declares that Lloyd's Register of Shipping is duly authorised by the said Government to issue this certificate.

Lloyd's Register of Shipping
71 Fenchurch Street, London EC3M 4BS

[1] For Oil tankers/Chemical tankers and Gas carriers only. [2] Delete as appropriate.
[3] Date on which keel was laid or ship was at a similar stage of construction or, where applicable, date on which work for a conversion or an alteration or modification of a major character was commenced.

FORM 1701 (11/91) 1/2

N°:
Page 2 of 2

MANDATORY ANNUAL SURVEYS

This is to certify that the ship has been surveyed in accordance with regulation I/6(b) of the Convention, as modified by the 1978 Protocol and the relevant recommendations of the Organisation[4].

1st mandatory annual survey *Date*

Place of survey *Surveyor to Lloyd's Register of Shipping*

2nd mandatory annual survey[5] *Date*

Place of survey *Surveyor to Lloyd's Register of Shipping*

3rd mandatory annual survey[5] *Date*

Place of survey *Surveyor to Lloyd's Register of Shipping*

4th mandatory annual survey *Date*

Place of survey *Surveyor to Lloyd's Register of Shipping*

INTERMEDIATE SURVEY FOR TANKERS OF 10 YEARS OF AGE AND OVER

This is to certify that, at an intermediate survey required by regulation I/10 of the Convention, as modified by the 1978 Protocol, this ship was found to comply with the relevant provisions of the Convention[4].

Intermediate survey *Date*

Place of survey *Surveyor to Lloyd's Register of Shipping*

[4] Reference is made to the Guidelines on surveys required by the 1978 SOLAS Protocol, the International Bulk Chemical Code and the International Gas Carrier Code adopted by the Organisation by resolution A.560(14).
[5] An intermediate survey may take the place of a mandatory annual survey.

FORM 1701 (11/91) 2/2

Lloyd's Register of Shipping

No ....

INTERNATIONAL LOAD LINE CERTIFICATE (1966)

Issued under the provisions of the

International Convention on Load Lines, 1966,

under the authority of the Government of

Name of Ship	Distinctive Number or Letters	Port of Registry	Length (L) as defined in Article 2(8)

Freeboard assigned as: *A new ship/*An existing ship   Type of ship: *Type A/*Type B with *reduced/*increased freeboard

	Freeboard from Deck Lline		Load Line	
Tropical	....	mm (T)	....	mm above (S)
Summer	....	mm (S)	Upper edge of line through centre of ring	
Winter	....	mm (W)	....	mm below (S)
Winter North Atlantic	....	mm (WNA)	....	mm below (S)
Timber Tropical	....	mm (LT)	....	mm above (LS)
Timber Summer	....	mm (LS)	....	mm above (S)
Timber Winter	....	mm (LW)	....	mm below (LS)
Timber Winter North Atlantic	....	mm (LWNA)	....	mm below (LS)

Note: Freeboards and Load Lines which are not applicable need not be entered on the certificate.

Allowance for Fresh Water for all freeboards other than timber .... mm

Allowance for Fresh Water for timber freeboards .... mm

The upper edge of the deck line from which these freeboards are measured is .... mm

....

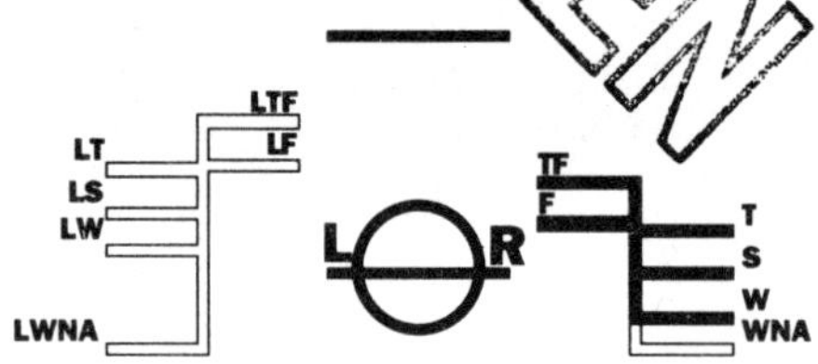

Date of initial or periodical survey

This is to certify that this ship has been surveyed and that the freeboards have been assigned and load lines shown above have been marked in accordance with the international Convention on Load Lines, 1966.

This certificate is valid until
subject to periodical inspections in accordance with Article 14(1)(c) of the Convention

Issued at   on

The undersigned declares that Lloyd's Register of Shipping is duly authorised by the said Government to issue this certificate.

....

Lloyd's Register of Shipping
71 Fenchurch Street, London EC3M 4BS

*Delete whatever is applicable

FORM 1241 (11/89)

This is to certify that at a periodical inspection required by Article 14(1)(c) of the Convention, this ship was found to comply with the relevant provisions of the Convention

Place .... Date ....

....

Surveyor to Lloyd's Register of Shipping

Place .... Date ....

....

Surveyor to Lloyd's Register of Shipping

Place .... Date ....

....

Surveyor to Lloyd's Register of Shipping

Place .... Date ....

....

Surveyor to Lloyd's Register of Shipping

The provisions of the Convention being fully complied with by this ship, the validity of this certificate is, in accordance with Article 19(2) of the Convention, extended until

Place .... Date ....

....

Surveyor to Lloyd's Register of Shipping

Notes:

1. When a ship departs from a port situated on a river or inland waters, deeper loading shall be permitted corresponding to the weight of fuel and all other materials required for consumption between the point of departure and the sea.
2. When a ship is in fresh water of unit density the appropriate load line may be submerged by the amount of the fresh water allowance shown above. Where the density is other than unity, an allowance shall be made proportional to the difference between 1.025 and the actual density.
3. This certificate must be kept framed and posted up in some conspicuous place on board the ship, so long as the certificate remains in force and the ship is in use.
4. Article 14(1)(c):
   A periodical inspection within three months either way of each annual anniversary date of the certificate, to ensure that alterations have not been made to the hull or superstructure which would affect the calculations determining the position of the load line and so as to ensure the maintenance in an effective condition of fittings and appliances for:
   - (i) protection of openings;
   - (ii) guard rails;
   - (iii) freeing ports; and
   - (iv) means of access to crew's quarters.

FORM 1241-1 (11/89)

Lloyd's Register of Shipping

INTERNATIONAL OIL POLLUTION PREVENTION CERTIFICATE

Issued under the provisions of the International Convention for the Prevention of Pollution from Ships, 1973, as modified by the Protocol of 1978 relating thereto (hereinafter referred to as 'the Convention') under the authority of the Government of

by Lloyd's Register of Shipping.

Name of Ship	Distinctive Number or Letters	Port of Registry	Gross Tonnage

Type of ship:

☐ *Oil tanker

☐ *Ship other than an oil tanker with cargo tanks coming under Regulation 2(2) of Annex I of the Convention

☐ *Ship other than any of the above

This is to certify:

1. That the ship has been surveyed in accordance with Regulation 4 of Annex I of the Convention; and

2. That the survey shows that the structure, equipment, systems, fittings, arrangement and material of the ship and the condition thereof are in all respects satisfactory and that the ship complies with the applicable requirements of Annex I of the Convention.

This Certificate is valid until..subject to surveys in accordance with Regulation 4 of Annex I of the Convention

Issued at London on..(date)

Date of Initial/Periodical survey..

....

Lloyd's Register of Shipping
71, Fenchurch Street, London EC3M 4BS

Note: This Certificate must be supplemented by a Record of Construction and Equipment.

*Mark box if applicable

Form 1465a (01/83)

ENDORSEMENT FOR ANNUAL AND INTERMEDIATE SURVEYS

This is to certify that at a survey required by Regulation 4 of Annex I of the Convention, the ship was found to comply with the relevant provisions of the Convention.

Place.. Date..

Annual Survey

....

Surveyor to Lloyd's Register of Shipping

Place.. Date..

*Annual/Intermediate Survey

....

Surveyor to Lloyd's Register of Shipping

Place.. Date..

*Annual/Intermediate Survey

....

Surveyor to Lloyd's Register of Shipping

Place.. Date..

Annual Survey

....

Surveyor to Lloyd's Register of Shipping

*Delete as appropriate

No. ....

Lloyd's Register of Shipping

INTERNATIONAL LOAD LINE CERTIFICATE (1966)

Issued under the provisions of the International Convention on Load Lines, 1966, under the authority of the

GOVERNMENT OF THE BAHAMAS

Name of Ship	Distinctive number or letters	Port of Registry	Length (L) as defined in Art. 2 (8)

Freeboard assigned as: *A new ship, *An existing ship

Type of Ship: *Type A, *Type B with *reduced/*increased freeboard

**Delete whatever is inapplicable*

Freeboard from Deck Line	Load Line
Tropical..mm (T)	....mm above (S)
Summer..mm (S)	Upper edge of line through centre of ring
Winter..mm (W)	....mm below (S)
Winter North Atlantic..mm (WNA)	....mm below (S)
Timber Tropical..mm (LT)	....mm above (LS)
Timber Summer..mm (LS)	....mm above (S)
Timber Winter..mm (LW)	....mm below (LS)
Timber Winter North Atlantic..mm (LWNA)	....mm below (LS)

Note: Freeboards and Load Lines which are not applicable need not be entered on the certificate.

Allowance for Fresh Water for all freeboards other than timber..mm

Allowance for Fresh Water for timber freeboards..mm

The upper edge of the deck line from which these freeboards are measured is..mm

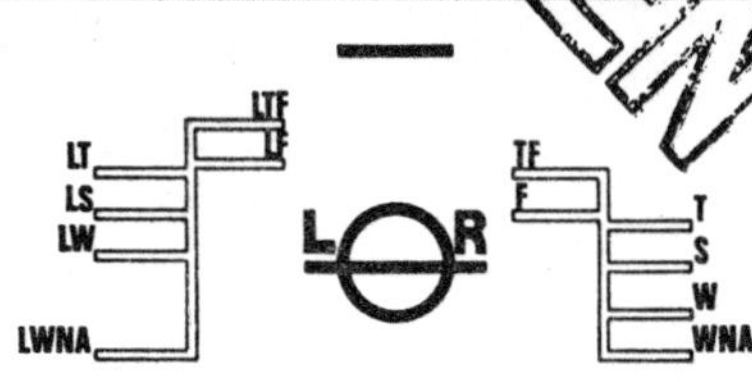

Date of initial or periodical survey..

This is to certify that this ship has been surveyed and that the freeboards have been assigned and load lines shown above have been marked in accordance with the International Convention on Load Lines, 1966.

This certificate is valid until.., subject to periodical inspections in accordance with Article 14(1)(c) of the Convention.

Issued at.. on..19.................

The undersigned declares that Lloyd's Register of Shipping is duly authorised by the said Government to issue this certificate.

....

Lloyd's Register of Shipping,
71, Fenchurch Street, London, EC3M 4BS

Form 1178 (9/76)

This is to certify that at a periodical inspection required by Article 14(1)(c) of the Convention, this ship was found to comply with the relevant provisions of the Convention.

Place.. Date..

....

Surveyor to Lloyd's Register of Shipping

Place.. Date..

....

Surveyor to Lloyd's Register of Shipping

Place.. Date..

....

Surveyor to Lloyd's Register of Shipping

Place.. Date..

....

Surveyor to Lloyd's Register of Shipping

The provisions of the Convention being fully complied with by this ship, the validity of this certificate is, in accordance with Article 19(2) of the Convention, extended until..

Place.. Date..

....

Lloyd's Register of Shipping

Notes:

1. When a ship departs from a port situated on a river or inland waters, deeper loading shall be permitted corresponding to the weight of fuel and all other materials required for consumption between the point of departure and the sea.

2. When a ship is in fresh water of unit density the appropriate load line may be submerged by the amount of the fresh water allowance shown above. Where the density is other than unity, an allowance shall be made proportional to the difference between 1.025 and the actual density.

3. This certificate is to be framed and posted up in some conspicuous place on board the ship, so long as the certificate remains in force and the ship is in use.

4. Article 14(1) (c):
A periodical inspection within three months either way of each annual anniversary date of the certificate, to ensure that alterations have not been made to the hull or superstructure which would affect the calculations determining the position of the load line and so as to ensure the maintenance in an effective condition of fittings and appliances for:
   (i) protection of openings;
   (ii) guard rails;
   (iii) freeing ports; and
   (iv) means of access to crew's quarters.

Lloyd's Register of Shipping

No.......................

CERTIFICADO INTERNACIONAL DE FRANCOBORDO (1966)

INTERNATIONAL LOAD LINE CERTIFICATE (1966)

Expedido en virtud de las disposiciones del Convenio Internacional de 1966, sobre Líneas de Carga, en nombre del Gobierno de la República de Panamá, por la Lloyd's Register of Shipping.

Issued under the provisions of the International Convention on Load Lines, 1966, under the authority of the Government of the Republic of Panama by Lloyd's Register of Shipping.

Nombre del Buque *Name of ship*	Número o letras distintivas *Distinctive numeral or letters*	Puerto de registro *Port of Registry*	Eslora (L) definida en el artículo 2(8) *Length (L) as defined in Article 2 (8)*

Francobordo asignado como: *Buque neuvo *Buque existente
Freeboard assigned as: A new ship An existing ship
Tipo de buque: *Tipo A *Tipo B con francobordo reducido/*Tipo B con francobordo aumentado
*Type of ship: *Type A *Type B with *reduced/*increased freeboard*

*Tache lo que no corresponda
**Delete whatever is inapplicable*

Francobordo medido desde la línea de cubierta / *Freeboard from Deck Line* — Situación de la línea de carga / *Load Line*

Tropical / *Tropical* .... mm (T) .... mm por encima de (V) / *above (V)*

Verano / *Summer* .... mm (V) — Borde superior de la línea situado a la altura del centro del anillo / *Upper edge of line at the level of centre of ring*

Invierno / *Winter* .... mm (I) .... mm por debajo de (V) / *below (V)*

Atlántico Norte Invierno / *Winter North Atlantic* .... mm (ANI) .... mm por debajo de (V) / *below (V)*

Madera, Tropical / *Timber Tropical* .... mm (MT) .... mm por encima de (MV) / *above (MV)*

Madera, Verano / *Timber Summer* .... mm (MV) .... mm por encima de (V) / *above (V)*

Madera, Invierno / *Timber Winter* .... mm (MI) .... mm por debajo de (MV) / *below (MV)*

Madera, Atlántico Norte Invierno / *Timber Winter North Atlantic* .... mm (MANI) .... mm por debajo de (MV) / *below (MV)*

NOTA: Los francobordos y líneas de carga que no sean applicables no necesitan ser mencionados en el certificado.
***Note:** Freeboards and load lines which are not applicable need not be entered on the certificate.*

Reducción en agua dulce para todos los francobordos diferentes del de madera / *Allowance for fresh water for all freeboards other than timber* .... mm

Para el francobordo para madera / *For timber freeboards* .... mm

El borde superior de la marca de la línea de cubierta, desde el cual se miden estos francobordos está a .... mm
The upper edge of the deck line from which these freeboards are measured is

.... de la cubierta en el costado. / *deck at side*

SPECIMEN

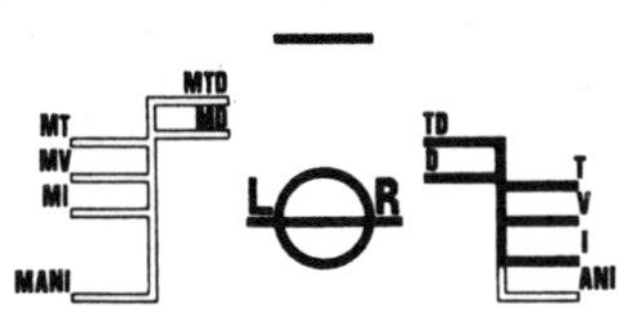

Se certifica que este buque ha sido visitado y que han sido asignados los francobordos y se han marcado las líneas de carga anteriormente indicadas de acuerdo con lo dispuesto en el Convenio Internacional sobre Líneas de Carga de 1966.

This is to certify that this ship has been surveyed and that the freeboards have been assigned and load lines shown above have been marked in accordance with the International Convention on Load Lines, 1966.

Fecha de la visita inicial o periódica ....
Date of initial or periodical survey

Este certificado es válido hasta .... sometido a inspecciones periódicas de conformidad con el Artículo 14 (1) (c) del Convenio.
This certificate is valid until .... subject to periodical inspections in accordance with Article 14 (1) (c) of the Convention.

Expedido en Londres el ....
(Fecha de expedición)
(Date of issue)

El infrascrito declará que la Lloyd's Register of Shipping está debidamente autorizado por dicho Gobierno para expedir este certificado.
The undersigned declares that Lloyd's Register of Shipping is duly authorised to issue this certificate.

(Sello de la Entidad que expide el certificado)
(Seal of issuing authority)

Notas: Véase al dorso
Notes: See Reverse of Certificate

....
Lloyd's Register of Shipping
71, Fenchurch Street, London, EC3M 4BS

Form 1254 (09/81)

NOTAS:

1. **Cuando un buque parta de un puerto situado en un rio o en aguas interiores, se le permitirá cargar hasta un calado mayor, correspondiente al peso de combustible y otras provisiones necesarias para el consumo entre el punto de salida y la mar.**

2. **Cuando un buque navegue en agua dulce de densidad igual a la unidad la linea de carga correspondiente podrá sumergirse en la cantidad correspondiente a la concesión para agua dulce indicada anteriormente. Cuando la densidad sea diferente de la unidad se hará una concesión proporcional a la diferencia entre 1,025 y la densidad real.**

NOTES:

1. ***When a ship departs from a port situated on a river or inland waters, deeper loading shall be permitted corresponding to the weight of fuel and all other materials required for consumption between the point of departure and the sea.***

2. ***When a ship is in fresh water of unit density the appropriate load line may be submerged by the amount of the fresh water allowance shown above. Where the density is other than unity, an allowance shall be made proportional to the difference between 1·025 and the actual density.***

Se certifica que en la inspección periódica prevista en el Artículo 14 (1) (c) del Convenio, este buque cumplía las prescripciones del Convenio.
This is to certify that at a periodical inspection required by Article 14 (1) (c) of the Convention, this ship was found to comply with the relevant provision's of the Convention.

En .... **Fecha** ....
Place ***Date***

Firma y sello del Inspector de Lloyd's Register of Shipping
Signature and Seal of the Surveyor to Lloyd's Register of Shipping

En .... **Fecha** ....
Place ***Date***

Firma y sello del Inspector de Lloyd's Register of Shipping
Signature and Seal of the Surveyor to Lloyd's Register of Shipping

En .... **Fecha** ....
Place ***Date***

Firma y sello del Inspector de Lloyd's Register of Shipping
Signature and Seal of the Surveyor to Lloyd's Register of Shipping

En .... **Fecha** ....
Place ***Date***

Firma y sello del Inspector de Lloyd's Register of Shipping
Signature and Seal of the Surveyor to Lloyd's Register of Shipping

Habiendo cumplido este buque por completo las prescripciones del Convenio, se prorroga la validez de este certificado, de acuerdo con el Artículo 19 (2) del Convenio, hasta ....

The provisions of the Convention being fully complied with by this ship, the validity of this certificate is, in accordance with Article 19 (2) of the Convention, extended until ....

En .... **Fecha** ....
Place ***Date***

Lloyd's Register of Shipping

Republic of Liberia

No.................

INTERNATIONAL LOAD LINE CERTIFICATE (1966)

Issued under the provisions of the International Convention on Load Lines, 1966, under the authority of the Government of the Republic of Liberia by Lloyd's Register of Shipping

Name of Ship	Distinctive number or letters	Port of Registry	Length (L) as defined in Art. 2 (8)

Freeboard assigned as: *A new ship *An existing ship

Type of ship: *Type A *Type B with *reduced/*increased/*timber freeboard

*Delete as applicable

Freeboard from Deck Line	Load Line
Tropical..................mm (T)	..................mm above (S)
Summer..................mm (S)	Upper edge of line through centre of ring
Winter..................mm (W)	..................mm below (S)
Winter North Atlantic..................mm (WNA)	..................mm below (S)
Timber Tropical..................mm (LT)	..................mm above (LS)
Timber Summer..................mm (LS)	..................mm above (S)
Timber Winter..................mm (LW)	..................mm below (LS)
Timber Winter North Atlantic..................mm (LWNA)	..................mm below (LS)

Note: Freeboards and Load Lines which are not applicable need not be entered in the certificate.

Allowance for Fresh Water for all freeboards other than timber..................mm

Allowance for Fresh Water for timber freeboards..................mm

The upper edge of the deck line from which these freeboards are measured is..................mm

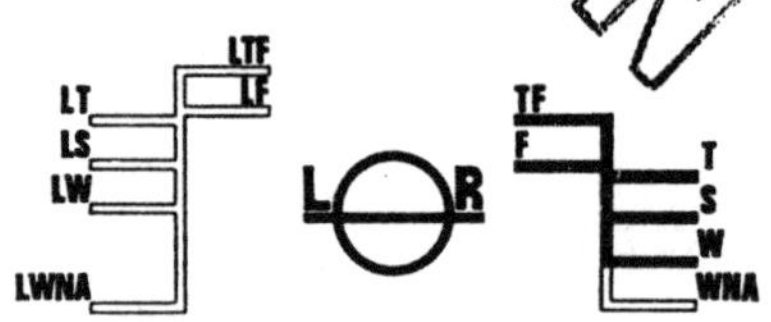

Date of initial or periodical survey..................

This is to certify that this ship has been surveyed and that the freeboards have been assigned and load lines shown above have been marked in accordance with the International Convention on Load Lines, 1966.

This certificate is valid until.................................., subject to periodical inspections in accordance with Article 14(1)(c) of the Convention.

Issued at London on..................

The undersigned declares that Lloyd's Register of Shipping is duly authorised by the said Government to issue this certificate.

....

Lloyd's Register of Shipping,
71 Fenchurch Street, London, EC3M 4BS

Form 1197 (11/80)

This is to certify that at a periodical inspection required by Article 14(1)(c) of the Convention, this ship was found to comply with the relevant provisions of the Convention.

Place.................................... Date....................................

....
Surveyor to Lloyd's Register of Shipping

Place.................................... Date....................................

....
Surveyor to Lloyd's Register of Shipping

Place.................................... Date....................................

....
Surveyor to Lloyd's Register of Shipping

Place.................................... Date....................................

....
Surveyor to Lloyd's Register of Shipping

The provisions of the Convention being fully complied with by this ship, the validity of this certificate is, in accordance with Article 19 (2) of the Convention, extended until....................................

Place.................................... Date....................................

....
Lloyd's Register of Shipping

Notes:

1. •When a ship departs from a port situated on a river or inland waters, deeper loading shall be permitted corresponding to the weight of fuel and all other materials required for consumption between the point of departure and the sea.
2. When a ship is in fresh water of unit density the appropriate load line may be submerged by the amount of the fresh water allowance shown above. Where the density is other than unity, an allowance shall be made proportional to the difference between 1·025 and the actual density.
3. This certificate must be kept framed and posted up in some conspicuous place on board the ship, so long as the certificate remains in force and the ship is in use.
4. Article 14(1)(c):
A periodical inspection within three months either way of each annual anniversary date of the certificate, to ensure that alterations have not been made to the hull or superstructure which would affect the calculations determining the position of the load line and so as to ensure the maintenance in an effective condition of fittings and appliances for:
    (i) protection of openings;
    (ii) guard rails;
    (iii) freeing ports; and
    (iv) means of access to crew's quarters.

No. ....

INTERNATIONAL LOAD LINE CERTIFICATE (1966)

Issued under the authority of the Government of Greece under the provisions of the International Convention on Load Lines, 1966, by Lloyd's Register of Shipping.

Name of Ship	Distinctive Number or Letters	Port of Registry	Ship's Length as defined in Art. 2 (8)

Freeboard assigned as: *A new ship *An existing ship
Type of Ship: *Type A *Type B with *reduced / *increased freeboard
*Delete whatever is inapplicable

Freeboard from Deck line		Load Line
Tropical	..........mm (T)	..........mm above (S)
Summer	..........mm (S)	Upper edge of line through centre of ring
Winter	..........mm (W)	..........mm below (S)
Winter North Atlantic	..........mm (WNA)	..........mm below (S)
Timber Tropical	..........mm (LT)	..........mm above (LS)
Timber Summer	..........mm (LS)	..........mm above (S)
Timber Winter	..........mm (LW)	..........mm below (LS)
Timber Winter North Atlantic	..........mm (LWNA)	..........mm below (LS)

Note: Freeboards and Load Lines which are not applicable need not be entered in the certificate.

Allowance for Fresh Water for all freeboards other than timber..........mm

Allowance for Fresh Water for timber freeboards..........mm

The upper edge of the deck line from which these freeboards are measured is..........mm

....

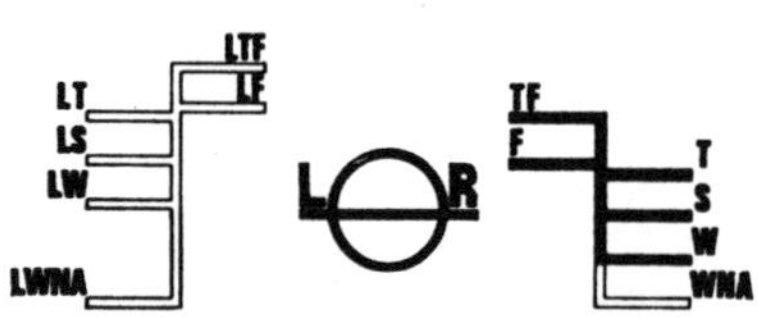

Date of initial or periodical survey..........

This is to certify that this ship has been surveyed and that the freeboards have been assigned and load lines shown above have been marked in accordance with the International Convention on Load Lines, 1966.

This certificate is valid until.........., subject to periodical inspections in accordance with Article 14 (1) (c) of the Convention.

Issued at London on..........

The undersigned declares that Lloyd's Register of Shipping is duly authorised by the said Government to issue this certificate.

....
Lloyd's Register of Shipping
71 Fenchurch Street, London, EC3M 4BS

Form 1330 (07/81)

This is to certify that at a periodical inspection required by Article 14(1) (c) of the Convention, this ship was found to comply with the relevant provisions of the Convention.

Place............................ Date............................

....
Signature of Surveyor

Place............................ Date............................

....
Signature of Surveyor

Place............................ Date............................

....
Signature of Surveyor

Place............................ Date............................

....
Signature of Surveyor

The provisions of the Convention being fully complied with by this ship, the validity of this certificate is, in accordance with Article 19 (2) of the Convention, extended until ....

Place............................ Date............................

....
Lloyd's Register of Shipping

Notes:

1. When a ship departs from a port situated on a river or inland waters, deeper loading shall be permitted corresponding to the weight of fuel and all other materials required for consumption between the point of departure and the sea.

2. When a ship is in fresh water of unit density the appropriate load line may be submerged by the amount of the fresh water allowance shown above. Where the density is other than unity, an allowance shall be made proportional to the difference between 1·025 and the actual density.

NO. ....

ΔΙΕΘΝΕΣ ΠΙΣΤΟΠΟΙΗΤΙΚΟΝ ΓΡΑΜΜΗΣ ΦΟΡΤΩΣΕΩΣ 1966

'Εκδοθέν κατ' ἐξουσιοδότησιν τῆς 'Ελληνικῆς Κυβερνήσεως συμφώνως πρός τάς διατάξεις τῆς Διεθνοῦς Συμβάσεως περί Γραμμῆς Φορτώσεως 1966 ὑπό Lloyd's Register of Shipping.

Ονομα Πλοιου	Διακριτικος Αριθμοςρ ἤ Γραμματα	Λιμην Νηολογησεως	Μηκος Πλοιου ως καθοριζεται εις Αρθρ. 2(8)

Ὕψος ἐξάλων προσδιορισθέν ὡς νέον πλοῖον/ὑπᾶρχον πλοῖον
Τύπος πλοίου: Τύπος Α, τύπος Β μέ ἠλαττωμένον/ηὐξημένον ὕψος ἐξάλων } *Νά διαγραφῇ ὁπουδήποτε μή ἐφαρμόσιμον*

«Διά στοιχεία βλέπε 'Αγγλικήν μετάφρασιν»

Ὕψος ἐξάλων ἀπό γραμμῆς καταστρώματος		Γραμμή Φορτώσεως
Τροπικόν	χιλσμ. (Τ)	.... χιλσμ. ὕπερθεν (Θ)
Θέρους	χιλσμ. (Θ)	Ἄνω ἀκμή τῆς διά τοῦ κέντρου τοῦ δίσκου γραμμῆς
Χειμῶνος	χιλσμ. (Χ)	.... χιλσμ. κάτωθεν (Θ)
Χειμῶνος Β. 'Ατλαντικοῦ	χιλσμ. (ΧΒΑ)	.... χιλσμ. κάτωθεν (Θ)
Τροπικόν Ξυλείας	χιλσμ. (ΞΤ)	.... χιλσμ. ὕπερθεν (ΞΘ)
Θέρους Ξυλείας	χιλσμ. (ΞΘ)	.... χιλσμ. ὕπερθεν (Θ)
Χειμῶνος Ξυλείας	χιλσμ. (ΞΧ)	.... χιλσμ. κάτωθεν (ΞΘ)
Χειμῶνος Β. 'Ατλαντικοῦ Ξυλείας	χιλσμ (ΞΧΒΑ)	.... χιλσμ. κάτωθεν (ΞΘ)

Σημείωσις: Ὕψος ἐξάλων καί γραμμαί φορτώσεως αἱ ὁποῖαι δέν ἐφαρμόζονται δέν ἀπαιτεῖται νά ἐγγραφοῦν ἐπί τοῦ Πιστοποιητικοῦ.

'Ανοχή γλυκέος ὕδατος δι' ἅπαντα τά ὕψη ἐξάλων ἐκτός τῆς ξυλείας .... χιλσμ.

'Ανοχή γλυκέος ὕδατος διά τό ὕψος ἐξάλων ξυλείας .... χιλσμ.

'Η ἄνω ἀκμή τῆς γραμμῆς καταστρώματος ἀφ' ἧς ἐμετρήθησαν τά ἀνωτέρω ὕψη ἐξάλων εὑρίσκεται .... χιλσμ. ....
.... καταστρώματος εἰς τήν πλευράν τοῦ πλοίου.

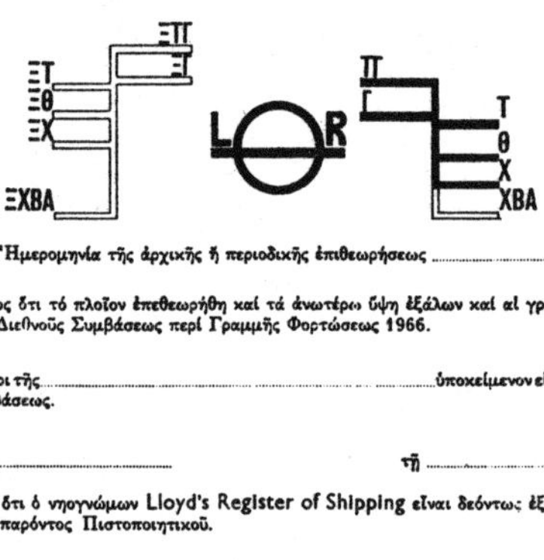

'Ημερομηνία τῆς ἀρχικῆς ἤ περιοδικῆς ἐπιθεωρήσεως ....

Πιστοποιεῖται διά τοῦ παρόντος ὅτι τό πλοῖον ἐπεθεωρήθη καί τά ἀνωτέρω ὕψη ἐξάλων καί αἱ γραμμαί φορτώσεως προσδιωρίσθησαν συμφώνως πρός τάς Διατάξεις τῆς Διεθνοῦς Συμβάσεως περί Γραμμῆς Φορτώσεως 1966.

Τό παρόν Πιστοποιητικόν ἰσχύει μέχρι τῆς .... ὑποκείμενον εἰς περιοδικάς ἐπιθεωρήσεις συμφώνω πρός τό ἄρθρον 14(1) (c) τῆς Συμβάσεως.

'Εξεδόθη ἐν .... τῇ .... 19........

'Ο κάτωθι ὑπογεγραμμένος δηλοῖ ὅτι ὁ νηογνώμων Lloyd's Register of Shipping εἶναι δεόντως ἐξουσιοδοτημένος ὑπό τῆς 'Ελληνικῆς Κυβερνήσεως διά τήν ἔκδοσιν τοῦ παρόντος Πιστοποιητικοῦ.

....
Lloyd's Register of Shipping
71 Fenchurch Street, London, EC3M 4BS

Πιστοποιεῖται ὅτι εἰς περιοδικὴν ἐπιθεώρησιν ἀπαιτουμένην ὑπό τοῦ ἄρθρου 14(1) (c) τῆς Συμβάσεως, τό παρόν πλοῖον εὑρέθη νά συμμορφοῦται μέ τάς σχετικάς διατάξεις τῆς Συμβάσεως.

Τόπος ____________ 'Ημερομ. ____________

....

'Υπογραφή 'Επιθεωρητοῦ

Τόπος ____________ 'Ημερομ. ____________

....

'Υπογραφή 'Επιθεωρητοῦ

Τόπος ____________ 'Ημερομ. ____________

....

'Υπογραφή 'Επιθεωρητοῦ

Τόπος ____________ 'Ημερομ. ____________

....

'Υπογραφή 'Επιθεωρητοῦ

'Εφ' ὅσον αἱ διατάξεις τῆς Συμβάσεως ἔχουν πλήρως τηρηθῆ ὑπό τοῦ παρόντος πλοίου, ἡ ἰσχύς τοῦ παρόντος Πιστοποιητικοῦ συμφώνως πρός τό ἄρθρον 19(2) τῆς Συμβάσεως παρατείνεται μέχρι ____________

Τόπος ____________ 'Ημερομ. ____________

....

Lloyd's Register of Shipping

Παρατηρήσεις:

1. Ὅταν ἕν πλοῖον ἀποπλέει ἐκ λιμένος εὑρισκομένου ἐπί ποταμοῦ ἤ μεσογείων ὑδάτων ἐπιτρέπεται ὑπερφόρτωσις ἀνταποκρινομένη εἰς τό βάρος τοῦ καυσίμου καί ὅλων τῶν ἄλλων ὑλικῶν, τό ἀπαιτούμενον διά τήν κατανάλωσιν μεταξύ τοῦ σημείου τῆς ἀναχωρήσεως καί τῆς θαλάσσης.

2. Ὅταν ἕν πλοῖον εὑρίσκεται εἰς γλυκύ ὕδωρ πυκνότητος ἴσης μέ τήν μονάδα ἡ κανονική γραμμή φορτώσεως δύναται νά βυθισθῆ κατ τό ποσόν τῆς ἀνοχῆς γλυκέος ὕδατος τό δεικνυόμενον ἀνωτέρω. Ὅταν ἡ πυκνότης εἶναι διάφορος τῆς μονάδος, ἡ ἀνοχή θά εἶναι ἀνάλογος πρός τήν διαφοράν μεταξύ 1,025 καί τῆς πραγματικῆς πυκνότητος.

Lloyd's Register of Shipping
71 Fenchurch Street
London EC3M 4BS
Telephone 071-709 9166
Telex 888379 LR LON G
Fax 071-488 4796

Our ref FSD/CONF/

Your ref

Date

SPECIMEN

CONFIRMATION OF CLASS

This is to certify that, according to current information available in this office, the Class Status of the undermentioned ship/unit is as follows:

L.R. Number

Name of Ship/Unit

Gross Tonnage

Date of Build

Class Status

Issuing Office

Lloyd's Register

NOTICE - This document is subject to the terms and conditions overleaf, which form part of this document.

FORM 1437 (10/90) Lloyd's Register of Shipping, registered office: 71 Fenchurch Street, London EC3M 4BS

Terms and Conditions

Maintenance of Class is subject to compliance with the requirements of Lloyd's Register of Shipping's (LR's) Rules and Regulations.

In providing services information or advice neither LR nor any of its employees or agents warrants the accuracy of any information or advice supplied. Except as set out herein neither LR nor any of its employees or agents (on behalf of each of whom LR has agreed this clause) shall be liable for any loss damage or expense whatever sustained by any person due to any act or omission or error of whatsoever nature and howsoever caused of LR its employees or agents or due to any inaccuracy of whatsoever nature and howsoever caused in any information or advice given in any way whatsoever by or on behalf of LR, even if held to amount to a breach of warranty. Nevertheless, if any person who is a party to the agreement pursuant to which this certificate is issued uses LR's services or relies on any information or advice given by or on behalf of LR and suffers loss damage or expense thereby which is proved to have been due to any negligent act omission or error of LR its employees or agents or any negligent inaccuracy in information or advice given by or on behalf of LR then LR will pay compensation to such person for his proved loss up to but not exceeding the amount of the fee (if any) charged by LR for that particular service information or advice.

LR its employees and agents (on behalf of whom this notice is given) shall be under no liability or responsibility in negligence or otherwise howsoever to any person who is not a party to the agreement pursuant to which this certificate is issued in respect of any information or advice expressly or impliedly given by or in this certificate or in respect of any omission or inaccuracy herein or in respect of any act or omission which has caused or contributed to this certificate being issued with the information and advice it contains (if any).

Lloyd's Register

LLOYD'S REGISTER FOUNDED 1760

NOTICE – This certificate is subject to the terms and conditions overleaf, which form part of this certificate.

FORM 1124 (10/92) Lloyd's Register of Shipping, registered office: 71 Fenchurch Street, London EC3M 4BS

TERMS AND CONDITIONS

In providing services, information or advice, neither Lloyd's Register of Shipping (hereinafter referred to as 'LR') nor any of its officers, employees or agents warrants the accuracy of any information or advice supplied. Except as set out herein, neither LR nor any of its officers, employees or agents (on behalf of each of whom LR has agreed this clause) shall be liable for any loss, damage or expense whatever sustained by any person due to any act, omission or error of whatsoever nature and howsoever caused of LR, its officers, employees or agents or due to any inaccuracy of whatsoever nature and howsoever caused in any information or advice given in any way whatsoever by or on behalf of LR, even if held to amount to a breach of warranty. Nevertheless, if any person who is party to the agreement pursuant to which LR provides any service, uses LR's services or relies on any information or advice given by or on behalf of LR and suffers loss, damage or expense thereby which is proved to have been due to any negligent act, omission or error of LR, its officers, employees or agents or any negligent inaccuracy in information or advice given by or on behalf of LR, then LR will pay compensation to such person for his proved loss up to but not exceeding the amount of the fee (if any) charged by LR for that particular service, information or advice.

LR, its officers, employees and agents (on behalf of each of whom this notice is given) shall be under no liability or responsibility in negligence or otherwise howsoever to any person who is not a party to the agreement with LR pursuant to which any certificate, statement, data or report is issued in respect of any information or advice expressly or impliedly given by LR or in respect of any omission or inaccuracy therein or in respect of any act or omission which has caused or contributed to any certificate, statement, data or report being issued with the information and advice it contains (if any).

Nº:
Page 1 of 2

Lloyd's Register

Cargo Ship Safety Equipment Certificate

This Certificate shall be supplemented by a Record of Equipment (Form E), Nº:

Issued under the provisions of the International Convention for the Safety of Life at Sea, 1974, as amended (hereinafter referred to as 'the Convention') under the authority of the Government of

Particulars of Ship

Name of ship
Distinctive number or letters
Port of registry
Gross tonnage
Deadweight of ship (metric tons)[1]
Length of ship (regulation III/3.10)
IMO Number
Type of Ship: Oil tanker[2] / Chemical tanker[2] / Gas carrier[2] / Cargo ship other than any of the above[2]
Date on which keel was laid[3]

This is to certify:

1. that the ship has been surveyed in accordance with the requirements of regulation I/8 of the Convention;
2. that the survey showed that:
   - 2.1 the ship complied with the requirements of the Convention as regards fire safety systems and appliances and fire control plans;
   - 2.2 the life-saving appliances and the equipment of the lifeboats, liferafts and rescue boats were provided in accordance with the requirements of the Convention;
   - 2.3 the ship was provided with a line-throwing appliance and radio installations used in life-saving appliances in accordance with the requirements of the Convention;
   - 2.4 the ship complied with the requirements of the Convention as regards shipborne navigational equipment, nautical publications and means of embarkation for pilots;
   - 2.5 the ship was provided with lights, shapes, means of making sound signals and distress signals in accordance with the requirements of the Convention and the International Regulations for Preventing Collisions at Sea in force;
   - 2.6 in all other respects the ship complied with the relevant requirements of the Convention;

[1] For Oil tankers/Chemical tankers and Gas carriers only. [2] Delete as appropriate.
[3] Date on which keel was laid or ship was at a similar stage of construction or, where applicable, date on which work for a conversion or an alteration or modification of a major character was commenced.

FORM 1704 (11/91) 1/2

Nº:
Page 2 of 2

3. that the ship operates in accordance with regulation III/26.1.1.1 within the limits of the trade area:

4. that an Exemption Certificate has / has not[2] been issued;

5. that a Lloyd's Register of Shipping Document of Compliance in accordance with regulation 54 of chapter II-2 for ships carrying dangerous goods has/has not[2] been issued.

This certificate is valid until

Issued at on

The undersigned declares that Lloyd's Register of Shipping is duly authorised by the said Government to issue this certificate.

Lloyd's Register of Shipping
71 Fenchurch Street, London EC3M 4BS

[2] Delete as appropriate.

FORM 1704 (11/91) 2/2

Nº:
Page 1 of 2

Lloyd's Register

Cargo Ship Safety Construction Certificate

Issued under the provisions of the International Convention for the Safety of Life at Sea, 1974, as amended (hereinafter referred to as 'the Convention') under the authority of the Government of

Particulars of Ship

Name of ship

Distinctive number or letters

Port of registry

Gross tonnage

Deadweight of ship (metric tons)[1]

IMO Number

Type of Ship: Oil tanker[2] / Chemical tanker[2] / Gas carrier[2] / Cargo ship other than any of the above[2]

Date on which keel was laid[3]

SPECIMEN

This is to certify:

1. that the ship has been surveyed in accordance with the requirements of regulation I/10 of the Convention;
2. that the survey showed that the condition of the structure, machinery and equipment as defined in the above regulation was satisfactory and the ship complied with the relevant requirements of chapters II-1 and II-2 of the Convention (other than those relating to fire safety systems and appliances and fire control plans);
3. that an Exemption Certificate has / has not[2] been issued;
4. that a Lloyd's Register of Shipping Document of Compliance in accordance with regulation 54 of chapter II-2 for ships carrying dangerous goods has/has not[2] been issued.

This certificate is valid until

Issued at on

The undersigned declares that Lloyd's Register of Shipping is duly authorised by the said Government to issue this certificate.

Lloyd's Register of Shipping
71 Fenchurch Street, London EC3M 4BS

[1] For Oil tankers/Chemical tankers and Gas carriers only. [2] Delete as appropriate.
[3] Date on which keel was laid or ship was at a similar stage of construction or, where applicable, date on which work for a conversion or an alteration or modification of a major character was commenced.

FORM 1702 (11/91) 1/2

No:
Page 2 of 2

ANNUAL SURVEYS

This is to certify that the ship has been surveyed in accordance with Lloyd's Register's annual survey regulations, the requirements of which are equivalent, so far as is applicable, to regulation I/6(b) of the Convention, as modified by the 1978 Protocol and the relevant recommendations of the Organisation[4].

1st annual survey — *Date*

Place of survey — *Surveyor to Lloyd's Register of Shipping*

2nd annual survey[5] — *Date*

Place of survey — *Surveyor to Lloyd's Register of Shipping*

3rd annual survey[5] — *Date*

Place of survey — *Surveyor to Lloyd's Register of Shipping*

4th annual survey — *Date*

Place of survey — *Surveyor to Lloyd's Register of Shipping*

INTERMEDIATE SURVEY FOR TANKERS OF 10 YEARS OF AGE AND OVER

This is to certify that, at an intermediate survey required by Lloyd's Register's classification regulations, the requirements of which are equivalent to an intermediate survey required by regulation I/10 of the Convention, as modified by the 1978 Protocol, this ship was found to comply with the relevant Lloyd's Register regulations[4].

Intermediate survey — *Date*

Place of survey — *Surveyor to Lloyd's Register of Shipping*

[4] Reference is made to the Guidelines on surveys required by the 1978 SOLAS Protocol, the International Bulk Chemical Code and the International Gas Carrier Code adopted by the Organisation by resolution A.560(14).
[5] An intermediate survey may take the place of an annual survey.

FORM 1702 (11/91) 2/2

Lloyd's Register

CERTIFICATE OF CLASS
REFRIGERATED CARGO INSTALLATION

This is to certify that the

Lloyd's Register Number

Number of Refrigerated Cargo Chambers

Total Capacity

having been surveyed by the Society's Surveyors and reported by them to be in a fit and efficient condition in accordance with the Rules and Regulations of Lloyd's Register of Shipping, has been assigned the class:

SPECIMEN

Chairman

Secretary

Date of Issue

Lloyd's Register of Shipping
71 Fenchurch Street, London EC3M 4BS

NOTICE—This certificate is subject to the Terms and Conditions overleaf, which form part of this certificate.

TERMS AND CONDITIONS

Continuance of Class is subject to compliance with the requirements of the Society's Rules and Regulations.

In providing services information or advice neither the Society nor any of its servants or agents warrants the accuracy of any information or advice supplied. Except as set out herein neither the Society nor any of its servants or agents (on behalf of each of whom the Society has agreed this clause) shall be liable for any loss damage or expense whatever sustained by any person due to any act or omission or error of whatsoever nature and howsoever caused of the Society its servants or agents or due to any inaccuracy of whatsoever nature and howsoever caused in any information or advice given in any way whatsoever by or on behalf of the Society, even if held to amount to a breach of warranty. Nevertheless, if any person uses the Society's services or relies on any information or advice given by or on behalf of the Society and suffers loss damage or expense thereby which is proved to have been due to any negligent act omission or error of the Society its servants or agents or any negligent inaccuracy in information or advice given by or on behalf of the Society then the Society will pay compensation to such person for his proved loss up to but not exceeding the amount of the fee (if any) charged by the Society for that particular service information or advice.

The Society, its officers servants and agents (on behalf of whom this notice is given) shall be under no liability or responsibility in negligence or otherwise howsoever to any person who is not a party to the agreement pursuant to which this certificate is issued in respect of any information or advice expressly or impliedly given by or in this certificate or in respect of any omission or inaccuracy herein or in respect of any act or omission which has caused or contributed to this certificate being issued with the information and advice it contains (if any).

Nº:
Page 1 of 1

Lloyd's Register

Exemption Certificate

Issued under the provisions of the International Convention for the Safety of Life at Sea, 1974, as amended (hereinafter referred to as 'the Convention') under the authority of the Government of

Particulars of Ship

Name of ship

Distinctive number or letters

Port of registry

Gross tonnage

IMO Number

This is to certify:

1. that the ship is, under the authority conferred by regulation of the Convention, exempted from the requirements of

   of the Convention.

2. Conditions, if any, for which the Exemption Certificate is granted:

3. Voyages, if any, for which the Exemption Certificate is granted:

This certificate is valid until

subject to the Certificate, to which

this certificate is attached, remaining valid.

Issued at on

The undersigned declares that Lloyd's Register of Shipping is duly authorised by the said Government to issue this certificate.

Lloyd's Register of Shipping
71 Fenchurch Street, London EC3M 4BS

FORM 1700 (11/91) 1/1

Lloyd's Register of Shipping

Certificate of Class

This is to certify **that the refrigerating plant and insulated chambers of the refrigerated store owned by**

having been built in accordance with the Rules for the Survey and Classification of Refrigerated Stores under the of the Society's Surveyors and reported by them on to be in a fit and efficient condition for the safe storage of refrigerated produce, the store has been assigned the class of in the Register Book subject to continued compliance with the requirements of the Society's Rules and Regulations.

Chairman

Secretary

Date of issue

Lloyd's Register of Shipping
71 Fenchurch Street, London EC3M 4BS

Lloyd's Register

Notice: This certificate is subject to the terms and conditions overleaf

TERMS AND CONDITIONS

If this certificate relates to type approval, it certifies that the prototype(s) of the products referred to herein has/have been tested in the presence of Lloyd's Register of Shipping's (hereinafter referred to as 'LR') surveyors and found to meet the applicable criteria for the use specified herein, it does not mean or imply approval for any other use, nor approval of any products designed or manufactured otherwise than in strict conformity with the said prototype(s).

In providing services information or advice neither LR nor any of its employees or agents warrants the accuracy of any information or advice supplied. Except as set out herein neither LR nor any of its employees or agents (on behalf of each of whom LR has agreed this clause) shall be liable for any loss damage or expense whatever sustained by any person due to any act or omission or error of whatsoever nature and howsoever caused of LR its employees or agents or due to any inaccuracy of whatsoever nature and howsoever caused in any information or advice given in any way whatsoever by or on behalf of LR, even if held to amount to a breach of warranty. Nevertheless, if any person uses LR's services or relies on any information or advice given by or on behalf of LR and suffers loss damage or expense thereby which is proved to have been due to any negligent act omission or error of LR its employees or agents or any negligent inaccuracy in information or advice given by or on behalf of LR then LR will pay compensation to such person for his proved loss up to but not exceeding the amount of fee (if any) charged by LR for that particular service information or advice.

LR its employees and agents (on behalf of whom this notice is given) shall be under no liability or responsibility in negligence or otherwise howsoever to any person who is not a party to the agreement pursuant to which this certificate is issued in respect of any information or advice expressly or impliedly given by or in this certificate or in respect of any omission or inaccuracy herein or in respect of any act or omission which has caused or contributed to this certificate being issued with the information and advice it contains (if any).

Lloyd's Register of Shipping

CERTIFICATE OF CLASS

Certificate No.

This is to certify that the refrigerated cargo installation of the Motorship

Lloyd's Register No. , having been surveyed by the Society's Surveyors in accordance with the requirements of the Rules and Regulations for and reported by them to be in a fit and efficient condition for the conveyance of refrigerated cargoes, continues to be classed in the Register Book subject to continued compliance with the requirements of the Society's Rules and Regulations.

The undermentioned notation has been made in the Society's Records:

for Secretary

(For and on behalf of the
Committee of Lloyd's Register of Shipping)

Date of issue

Lloyd's Register of Shipping
71 Fenchurch Street, London EC3M 4BS

Lloyd's Register

Notice: This certificate is subject to the terms and conditions overleaf

TERMS AND CONDITIONS

If this certificate relates to type approval, it certifies that the prototype(s) of the products referred to herein has/have been tested in the presence of Lloyd's Register of Shipping's (hereinafter referred to as 'LR') surveyors and found to meet the applicable criteria for the use specified herein, it does not mean or imply approval for any other use, nor approval of any products designed or manufactured otherwise than in strict conformity with the said prototype(s).

In providing services information or advice neither LR nor any of its employees or agents warrants the accuracy of any information or advice supplied. Except as set out herein neither LR nor any of its employees or agents (on behalf of each of whom LR has agreed this clause) shall be liable for any loss damage or expense whatever sustained by any person due to any act or omission or error of whatsoever nature and howsoever caused of LR its employees or agents or due to any inaccuracy of whatsoever nature and howsoever caused in any information or advice given in any way whatsoever by or on behalf of LR, even if held to amount to a breach of warranty. Nevertheless, if any person uses LR's services or relies on any information or advice given by or on behalf of LR and suffers loss damage or expense thereby which is proved to have been due to any negligent act omission or error of LR its employees or agents or any negligent inaccuracy in information or advice given by or on behalf of LR then LR will pay compensation to such person for his proved loss up to but not exceeding the amount of fee (if any) charged by LR for that particular service information or advice.

LR its employees and agents (on behalf of whom this notice is given) shall be under no liability or responsibility in negligence or otherwise howsoever to any person who is not a party to the agreement pursuant to which this certificate is issued in respect of any information or advice expressly or impliedly given by or in this certificate or in respect of any omission or inaccuracy herein or in respect of any act or omission which has caused or contributed to this certificate being issued with the information and advice it contains (if any).

Lloyd's Register of Shipping

CERTIFICATE OF CLASS

Certificate No.

This is to certify that the

LR No. , having been surveyed by LR's Surveyors and reported by them on
to be in a fit and efficient condition and in accordance with the Rules and Regulations for the Classification of Ships, continues with the class

in the Register Book subject to continued compliance with the requirements of the LR's Rules and Regulations for the Classification of Ships.
The undermentioned notations have been made in LR's Records:

Secretary
(For and on behalf of the Committee of Lloyd's Register of Shipping)

Date of Issue
71 Fenchurch Street, London EC3M 4BS

In providing services information or advice neither Lloyd's Register of Shipping (hereinafter referred to as 'LR') nor any of its officers employees or agents warrants the accuracy of any information or advice supplied. Except as set out herein neither LR nor any of its officers employees or agents (on behalf of each of whom LR has agreed this clause) shall be liable for any loss damage or expense whatever sustained by any person due to any act or omission or error of whatsoever nature and howsoever caused of LR its officers employees or agents or due to any inaccuracy of whatsoever nature and howsoever caused in any information or advice given in any way whatsoever by or on behalf of LR, even if held to amount to a breach of warranty. Nevertheless, if any person, who is party to the agreement pursuant to which LR provides any service, uses LR's services or relies on any information or advice given by or on behalf of LR and suffers loss damage or expense thereby which is proved to have been due to any negligent act omission or error of LR its officers employees or agents or any negligent inaccuracy in information or advice given by or on behalf of LR then LR will pay compensation to such person for his proved loss up to but not exceeding the amount of fee (if any) charged by LR for that particular service information or advice.

FORM 1004 (05/92)

INDEX